Hackproof in Eight Principles

Rob Hockey

Copyright © 2024 Rob Hockey

All rights reserved.

Disclaimer/Limit of Liability
All views expressed in this book are my own and do not represent the views of any current, or previous employer. No assumption should be made that I am referring to any specific employer or client, when I refer to a historical work-related episode. I have also tried to be fair with any tech companies I have mentioned. Technology suppliers are constantly in the public eye and get a mixed reception, which is sometimes unjustified, harsh and unfair. I have tried to keep those views out of this book. Generally, I am in support of the IT industry and would like to see everyone do well. If we can overcome the current security setbacks, such as the continuing success of online criminals. I do not consider myself adversely influenced by any political, commercial, or lobby groups. For those in IT, try to use this information with caution. This book is not an end user license, to implement these ideas in an irresponsible way, they should be used mindfully. Most of these ideas are known to the security industry but some may be new to you. I am not responsible if you have not thought through what you are doing or take the information here and make a bad outcome of it. The aim is to make things better. The author has taken some care and good deal of effort in living out and preparing for this book. But there is no guarantee given, or assumed, about the accuracy of the information contained in it. IT security is a developing and fast-moving industry, the information may not be correct everywhere and at all times. Seek professional help if you are unsure. The author is not liable for any losses associated with consequential, or other damages. No additional sales warranties may be created or extended from this work. You can quote me for education, or fun but do not depend on my words here for profit, unless we have a legally binding contract, that I am fully aware of.

ISBN:979-8-8793-8659-2

private key. User B also can also generate a private key for themselves and send me their public key, and I use it to encrypt the response and send the encrypted message back to User B, who decrypts it with her private key.

This is the basic principle of public key cryptography. The mathematics is what creates a one-way transform, that cannot be reversed. For a long time, it has been predicted that mathematicians will soon discover a way of reversing the equation, without using computer brute-force. But at the moment, the existence of such a mathematics breakthrough is only speculative. Therefore, RSA is also a candidate for hackproof. It has been around much longer than ten years.

Other potential examples and misnomers

As large numbers of organizations have moved their existing systems onto public cloud. To receive the benefits of cost management, scalability and support. The cloud vendors have been trying to add-on compelling technologies to win over sceptics and achieve better compliance results.

One such product is the AWS Nitro Enclave. Now AWS Nitro brand is the range of computing hardware that makes up the AWS hypervisor layer and associated data storage, networking, etc. AWS Nitro Enclaves is a neat addition to AWS EC2 instances, that I like to think are the equivalent of old data centre servers but in the cloud. With Nitro Enclaves, you get a hyper secure little corner of the server that no one knows anything about, not even Amazon. Anything that happens there is just for you to see and you can do anything you want and it is secure.

There are some really compelling use cases that you can create with it. But I do not have time to expand in this book. I would genuinely recommend that you look into it because it has the potential to do in the cloud, what I have tried to explain in Chapter 11. At the moment, I am not aware of too many organisations using it and no one seems to be talking about it that much. But maybe they should be.

Bitcoin wallets are a technology that have been around for a few years now. And there are some interesting videos on YouTube, by the ex-hacker turned security researcher, Joe Grand. Who uses his skills in hardware and software hacking to break into bitcoin wallets, both hardware and software apps on mobile phones. He has incredible success and it is exhilarating to watch him recover lost wallets and make really large amounts of money for his efforts. Although there are examples of bitcoin wallets having well known vulnerabilities, such as side-channel attacks to recover password. On the whole bitcoin hardware wallets do exhibit a stronger level of security, than other software equivalents. They could be added to the list of hackproof technology if there were not so many of them being lost and having to be broken into. It also makes the point that maybe sometimes technology can be too tough. Imagine a world where locksmiths could not break into your house, if you lost your keys. You would probably have to get bulldozers and flatten the house to get in. With the cost of portable miniature angle grinders being so low, having steel walls may become a good option.

Software that has stood the test of time is very rare. The nginx webserver did not have any security vulnerabilities for a number of years, until earlier last year (2023), when a couple of vulnerabilities were found. In most cases where a website is hacked it is not due to bug in the webserver application being present but is usually software built on top of nginx, which is probably a softer target. Nginx is another candidate for hackproof, although it has had a couple of recent issues.

SeL4 is based on the L4 microkernel, it does not use Intel/AMD or ARM architecture like most computers. Although the software is open source, it is used in military drones and all applications have to be custom written. It is the first and possibly only operating system, with a "formally verified and tested design" against the Evaluation Assurance Level (EAL) level 7 criteria. A standard of software assurance that was only dreamed of when it was first defined in the 1990s. At that point the generally most secure devices were firewall appliances. Most firewalls of that time were around level EAL3/4. Although the SeL4 implementation is verified against the design, there could be a major design weaknesses, making verification against design irrelevant. Also, any applications running on it would also need to be verified against a design too, to make any sense. But it is really impressive, so that is why I added it to the list.

There are a few things that could be considered to be hackproof and many other items probably exist that I don't know about or have forgotten but it gives you an idea of the sorts of technologies that might qualify as hackproof. But the prevailing theme is that there is product line A, that is useable and does not specialise in security. There is no product line B that is security specific. Those products do not appear to make it to market.

One appearance I do remember was the Blackphone, that was held up as solving a lot of the early emerging security issues with mobile phones. But it does not have the majority market share now. I think that demonstrates that security sales features and advantages, are purely something in the minds of security professionals. A security led marketing approach does not actually exist in the mainstream IT markets. It is a sweeping statement to say consumers are not buying based on security alone. But that it limits the options for those who really need security, in key places that it needs to exist. The prevalence of consumer IoT, marketed for business use, takes the market forces example one step further. ETSI standards for security in IoT devices are geared to manufacturers and their consumer products. Not business products. There is only one security for all, as I see it.

Technical constraints of hackproof

In this section we are going to visit the more technical reasons why hackproof technologies are unlikely to become a compelling choice, unless we are forced into using them. And lets hope that does not happen. Mostly the technical drive is about usability, or the lack of it. But first let's look at one of the major forces governing the technology that is available on the market.

Standardisation covers many aspects of society, such as house building, maritime law, space travel, car manufacturing and fireworks. But for some reason the security standards around IT security do not appear to be as effective as those around aircraft safety. With the exception of Industrial Control System (ICS) standard. I realise that safety and security are two different things. But airport security is also something that is usually quoted as excessive security. But I cannot remember any airplane hostage situations recently. But the Colonial Pipeline ransomware incident just popped into my head as I was thinking about a parallel in IT.

Technical standards usually involve getting together representatives from the major stakeholder groups. So with IT that is usually a group of young hopefuls from the big tech firms, some highbrow IT consumers from Fortune 500 companies and some academics, who also might work for the big tech companies. I have never been to one of these meetings, so I cannot tell you precisely what they are like but I have seen a lot of team photos and delegate lists.

The standards body meets over several months of years and a standard is drafted that defines how the technology should be built. With some technologies, the supply and demand wave is so sudden, that it coalesces around a basic solution straight away and everyone gets on board. This is called a 'de facto' standard. Take for instance, multi-factor authentication. Yes, there are some standards, and it was around for at least ten years with mostly crypto keyrings and dongles, used by government, military and some banks. But suddenly it became very important around 2013 and then everyone started using One-Time Pad (OTP) over SMS text and email. Mobile authenticator apps suddenly became very widespread. None of this was as the result of a standards body as far as I know. The tech worked and people used it. There is some variation but not that could cause interoperability headaches in the main.

Standardisation and the Request for Comment (RFC) process are very useful for the way in which it ensures technologies are robust and the early developers think about every aspect of the design. Take for instance the Advanced Encryption Standard (AES) that superseded the Digital Encryption Standard (DES). Mostly, this has not caused any serious disruption and technology companies have been able to use the AES standard with confidence. There are no doubts over the effectiveness of it as a control.

On the contrary, take some control like a tamperproof seal. All technology (probably), depends on physical security at its heart. If an attacker can break into the building and open the casing, they might be able to tamper with the electronics and bypass all of the higher-level software controls. This is possible. But there are no robust standards for tamper proofing, that are common knowledge to the average member of the public. Although quite a lot of people have heard about AES256 encryption. The most we can expect from a technology vendor is a label that says, "Warranty Invalid if Removed" or something similar. I can imagine that there are plenty of those labels being pedalled on the black market. How difficult would it be to make a more effective tamperproof security control that the average person would be able to intuitively recognise that the equipment had been tampered with?

When trying to consider whether technology will ever be hackproof. I was asked the obvious question. What does hackproof technology look like? And it would be nice to say that its appearance is no different to the regular digital technologies that we are used to. But I think it would be fair to say that there might be a difference in appearance to begin with at least. The main one being the usability gap. With technologies as they currently are, the consumer, or businessperson has a general expectation of what technologies can be used for. With hackproof technologies, there are likely to be severe restrictions on functionality, being able to adjust settings, etc. So that is probably going to be the main set-back.

Hackproof will have to start with rewriting the physical and electronics of the device. If not to begin with, fairly soon that will be necessary as access by other means becomes less feasible. At some point, if hackproof ever did become a trend, there would need to be a re-adjustment by support providers because the service engineers would become a prime target for kidnapping as the only means of admin access perhaps? So personnel security would also need to increase. That may not be tolerable for some organisations, or engineers.

In chapter 11, there is a worked example of the kind of approach that might be used to develop hackproof technologies. Starting with basic principles, it will ask whether the device can be compromised in a number of ways and at various stages of any given attack, the attacker can use their standard techniques. The current techniques used by hackers are very few in basic functionality. The list on Mitre Attack framework is limited, if you remove all the possibilities from the Initial Compromise column, the rest of the columns become less of a potential threat and they too can be addressed as a layered approach. The following are the kinds of techniques that hackers rely upon to launch attacks: injecting malicious code into existing process through heap or stack memory, starting new threads within an existing process space, uninterrupted reverse network connections, starting new process, remote access to resources on the device, intercepting network traffic, abusing the way that web protocols work, bypassing server security checks, accessing credentials stored on device. For each of these attack types, there is a more robust process that can replace the existing way of implementation.

As previously mentioned, most hacking attacks will not write anything to disk, or start a new process if it can be helped. This means that that most of the time, the trojan will use higher level web technologies, or will be injected into an existing process space, as shellcode, or a new thread by calling a CreateThread() software function, or invoking a dynamic library call. There are ways of preventing this from happening. Which are likely to severely restrict hardware reuse or developer flexibility. But it is possible through configuration hardening, or task specific hardware, if the subroutine is built using ASICS chips. ASICS, or Application Specific Integrated Circuit, is a way of embedding a computer program in the form of electronics logic into the chipset. Instead of providing a multi-use microprocessor system, the ASICS only executes the program burnt into the silicon. It cannot do anything else. So in theory it cannot be hacked. Anyone who has done some ethical hacking will at this point be very sceptical as this is how most of the trouble starts. With some technology, that appears to be perfect in design, it very soon appears afterwards, that it is possible to use its functionality, in not so secure a way.

Take for instance a website that offers 30% discount vouchers. You use a perfectly hackproof webserver to post a 30% discount multiple times in a very short space of time and because the back-end database is not able to record the transactions quick enough. The amount payable is reduced to near zero. This is a real attack that has been seen recently with the advent of HTTP/2.0 state collision attacks. There is also the possibility for bypassing hackproof technologies with business logic issues. Hackproof technologies are just one pillar of the whole solution. The whole thing has to be tight. Also, hackproof technologies could be used by criminals. In fact, the main malware command and control servers used by gangs, such as Cobalt Strike, SOCKS and Brute Ratel, are also susceptible to vulnerabilities and must cause them endless stress, making sure they cannot be hacked by federal agents or rival criminals.

Not saying that a lot of thought and effort has not gone into developing modern web technologies. Almost certainly there are thousands of hours of core development work going on with the most used technologies. As web technologies have developed since the mid-nineties. The market has reconciled around a few technologies, the main client-side software being Google Chrome. The browser has about 60-70% of the market depending on whose figures you use.

But its open-source equivalent Chromium, is also built into desktop apps like Outlook, Slack, Visual Studio Code, Teams, and others. It is the runtime component of ElectronJS. During 2023, around 14 zero day exploits were found in Chromium/Chrome, which means that at any one point in time, the software was not completely unhackable. For all the bugs that were discovered, there was considerable effort in trying to find new bugs. Each year the Pwn2Own conference pits teams of hackers against each other and every year there are new bugs found in Chrome. This demonstrates that an effort of will and elite hacking skills, is all that is required to win the tens of thousands of dollars, available on the table for the latest mainstream exploits.

We will get onto the cash factor in this in the next chapter and that is unlikely to go away any time soon.

Chrome is a masterful work of market conquest, why would anyone use anything other than Chrome? I highly value its useability. There are a range of other browsers but they mostly use the same rendering engine software. Known as Apple Webkit, it was forked by Google, as the Blink rendering engine. Other rivals, have existed, such as the Gecko rendering engine, part of the Firefox browser and other Mozilla software. Internet Explorer has faded into obscurity over the past decade and Edge browser now also uses the Chromium renderer, as do other desktop applications. I use the Edge browser every day and it has some useful unique features, like the Collections bookmarking feature. Mobile devices also run the third-party browsers.

Considering there are more than a million lines of code in Chromium. The open-source project that sustains and is supported by the Chrome browser. Although open source is valuable for transparency, community development, it also allows hackers a clear view of what they need to do. The open-source idea is a choice in my view, that comes with a range of supporting options. You can choose closed source and that comes with a range of options too. It is a bold move to go public with your codebase, if you publish a majorly used piece of software. Take for instance the excellent messaging provider Threema, who decided after some years to make their codebase public. They came under some criticism after some routine software testing by a local university revealed a handful of security related issues. After a while, Threema decided to make all their code open source. Which I appreciate as a bold act of defiance, towards anyone who might think there are bugs in the code. Now everyone can see for themselves.

But in other cases, that has backfired. Especially where the open-source software is used in organisations handling sensitive data, that gets hacked. Each software vendor has to make a choice and so does the customer. Victory favours the bold.

Silent updates are providing a number of software installations with stealthy patching. In an age of ransomware, that makes no sense whatsoever, when you first hear it. Software installations, upgrades and patches have traditionally required some sort of user notification and manual action. But some updates recently are not involving the user at all. No notification, just a small spike in the CPU cycles and a couple of hundred megabytes of data downloaded. Mobile technology such as Feature Flags from companies like Telium, also provide the flexibility to enable sleeping functionality. Once the server-side capability has been finished, the client functionality can be enabled, without having to install a whole new version of a mobile app. There are merits and de-merits to involving the user in a corporate environment and I can accept that this may mean less service desk calls and emergency meetings.

The browser concept has grown over twenty-five years to first including scripting like ECMA, jscript and then making javascript and typescript all but mandatory in the contemporary browser. Apart from its use on the dark web, the browser requires javascript enabled to avoid breaking nearly every website you visit. Chapter 11 gives a worked example of a hackproof browser and there is no likelihood of this working with the website that currently exist. A major step back, in terms of website technology would be required to allow it to work. So, the replacement of one major part of the jigsaw, will have a interoperability effect on other components. We take interoperability for granted in the 2020s, but it was not like that during the 1990s. There were a series of exhibitions and working groups then that were marketed with such names as "Interop 1996", as far as I remember. To allow technology providers to understand what each other was doing and whether their equipment would work with other kit. Of course, the meeting had to be in person, so teams used to spend a number of days a year hanging out with each other, which also helped socialising and forming lifelong working alliances.

Javascript has become a new abstracted assembler language built on top of the browser, it uses the v8 pre-compiler to quickly compile scripts that need the additional efficiency that comes with compiled code. The javascript Domain Object Model is a fully featured set of programming objects and functions that allow the programmer free reign to design wonderful user interfaces.

The more recent advances in User Experience (UX) and interface design have led to technologies such as ReactJS that does not follow the same coding model as other languages. The programmer does not have to be exact about what it wants the program to do, just a general definition of what they want to achieve.

The implementation is dynamic and pre-empts the user's decisions by creating JavaScript-based webpages in advance of a user's decision to click on a link. It caches the potential choices. This takes various forms of implementation features, with names such as Server-Side Rendering, ISR, Client-Side Rendering and Rehydration. Each of these add complexity to the function of JavaScript in delivering content to the user and the fine art it has become, makes it harder for the possibility of replacing the foundational technologies that it is dependent on. In security, the choice should never be

"Do you want a beautiful interface, or something that is ultimately secure?" But there is context to take into consideration. A secure browser could be required for managing national critical infrastructure. Whereas checking the times at the local shops could be done on a regular browser. There are a range of use cases, and each one has a requirement for security and aesthetics.

Why does society appear to be blocking hackproof technologies?

Good Enough Security - some devops engineers use the term Minimal Viable Product, when developing a new application. It is the least amount of functionality that can be deployed to be called an application and it allows other features to be added over time, whilst users can start using the application with minimal features. 'Good Enough Security', is probably an equivalent term that could be used for the standard course of decision making in business, when choosing how secure to make a new system. For example, if you were to apply all of the security controls available to the business and spend a small fortune on software and technical hardware, it may still be possible to hack the application somehow. The business chooses to apply all the reasonably expected controls and then curb spending, when there is a security control tick-in-the-box for each section of the risk management spreadsheet. But controls are not effective in some cases and even multiple controls in the same category may not be enough. But if it comes to affecting useability and additional cost, businesses around the world will always choose the "Good Enough Security" option. I am not wrong in saying this. With the follow-up statement that we did all we could, and the certificates to prove it. Because what is the point of having a perfectly secure business system, if no-one is able to use it and dreads logging in every morning.

Supplier power dynamics - it may not sound like something that impacts security management. But there are a lot of cases in business life where the supplier has an unhealthy sway over purchasing decisions and also ongoing service delivery agreements. During the 17th Century the British East India Company controlled all imports from the Far East and similarly during the 19th Century the Hudson Bay Company controlled large swathes of North America. These were just incorporated companies, not nation states. But they had the equivalent soft power influence and guile to be able to do pretty much whatever they felt like. There are many tales of injustice and marauding commercial exploitation at the expense of ordinary people. Big tech companies, like medieval dynasties, operate at a similar power level. But the world is not the same as it was (Harry Styles) and now international regulation has the ability to impose fines on commercial superpowers. But the Latin phrase from business management text books 'Caveat Emptor', or 'Buyer Beware', still stands.

Big tech is driven by extreme pressures and appears to someone from the outside to be greedy and ruthless. But the constraints that it places on the progress of the security industry, are probably less than the pressure their executives receive, to increase profitability and deliver on new features. In general, I would imagine it is not a pleasant experience being a big tech executive. Something to think about before launching out in frustration at the latest choice that causes inconvenience.

One phenomenon that you also may have noted, with the release of new vulnerabilities in the past few years. Is a sort of "undertaker effect" of releasing a relentless number of serious vulnerabilities in one old product. That consequentially rings out the death knell. When the obvious solution is to move to the same vendor's SaaS equivalent product. This also makes me suspect, that given the right amount of motivation, security researchers can be made to find bugs in anything, if they look hard enough. The Pwn2Own events that are regularly held around the world, go some way to confirming this idea. Pwn2Own invites some of the best competitive hackers in the world to try and root compromise (pwn) all the latest big tech (iPhone, Android, Chrome, etc.) within a weekend conference setting. Mostly they hack all the things every time and win large cash bounties as a result, sometimes as much as a million dollars. So being able to play down old product lines as insecure is a convenient move that manufacturers may want to keep hold of.

Intelligence agencies and law enforcement - those who govern countries and keep the peace, need to be able to conduct investigations into criminal behaviour and control international situations. In a digital world, this means they need to access to other people's computers. During the Middle Ages, the local landowner would send the local sheriff around to break down a door. If they suspected one of the villagers of stealing. In many jurisdictions, this made way to search warrants in modern policing and in the UK, eventually the Regulation of Investigatory Powers Act (RIPA). But having the legal authority to act is not enough. The modest budgets of government agencies need to be able to afford cutting edge cyber weapons and experts. That does not come cheaply. The governments have motivation to keep the doors open to them.

One ongoing scheme that law enforcement and government agencies have been using for a number of years, is to be involved in the movement of high value vulnerabilities. When central security services discover a new bug, as well as disclosing it to the supplier, it might also find its way into their arsenal of cyber tools, for a fixed time window. That time window is dependent on a number of factors. I am not disclosing anything new here, this was first made public in a major way by whistleblowers around ten years ago. You can read about it in the interesting book by Nicole Perlroth titled "This is how they tell me the world ends". Since then, government sanctioned use of private vulnerabilities has become a very essential public service. But it has the effect of perpetuating the hackable over the hackproof. This is an ethical dilemma. Law enforcement and security services are superheroes but they can also suffer from the same technical frustrations as the rest of us. With things not working or being prevented from doing very necessary things to save human lives. Simply because of the necessary checks involve a lengthy process. When it comes to access for surveillance, to protect the nations and their commercial interests, there is a real need to get access when it is needed.

The haymaking process of retaining a few newly discovered vulnerabilities because they have not been discovered by someone else or been made public yet. The stress is on the "have not been made public" bit. It is completely possible that due to the weakening effect of holding back the security of technologies, others will get access that they should not be entitled to. This is a well understood idea within the global vulnerability disclosure circles but does not get much airplay with those outside the security industry.

What is the solution? Not sure I have an answer to giving access as well as making technology secure. Of course, if every criminal gang and security agency cannot get access, then they may have to use more conventional means of spying and tracking suspects. Maybe have a conversation with each other occasionally. If the hackproof paradigm involves task specific hardware implementations, that are not likely to be hacked within about ten years. The chances are that if a backdoor can be fitted or found. It is likely it has been there for a really long time. From what we are discussing here, I am confused as to whether that is a good idea or not.

Just at the start, when I first engaged with ideas about security technologies in 1998. Was around the time that the internet (Berners-Lee Web) was really kicking off and I was studying Computer Systems as University of Plymouth, in England. The digital electronics lectures led me to notice a debate going on in the journals, that maybe found some airplay in newspapers, obviously there was no social media, or real websites, as we would recognise them now. The US government was promoting the inclusion of key escrow, in new internet technologies, to allow the lawful interception of criminal communications. This meant that all comms equipment needed to have a specially fitted microchip, called the 'Clipper' chip. A bit like a car insurance black box. That would allow the US government to keep a copy of the encryption keys, used in business communications. From what I remember, there was a big backlash against the idea and in the end the move did not go ahead, as far as I remember they instead relied on the DES encryption standard and there were no further objections. I guess they could have offered a discount on the appliance if it had a Clipper chip? Insurance black telemetry box is very popular among young drivers.

Part of the reason that governments want to get access to public communications is because they need to know who the public enemies are. There seems to be some lack of vision when it comes to attacker attribution. When a cyber-attack happens, I have heard myself say something like "It was the Chinese". When what I mean is that it was a small team; part of a cyberwarfare unit, of the People's Liberation Army of China. Or it could have been a team of ex-military freelancers, led by Rick Johnson, backed by an international tycoon called Don Green and supported by two organised crime contacts, called Jim Smith and Leo Vitario. Apologies if you know anyone by these names, I was just making it up to make the point clearer. We want to know real names. The interception occurs to accelerate the investigation. To stop terrible things from happening. Real people do those things.

The generalisation is something we have got used to in the cyber security industry and attribution is always the last thing to arrive at. But always the first thing anyone wants to know. Who did it? That is one of the main questions we want to know. The nature of internet communication, when properly cloaked with the right anonymisation, means identification is the least likely thing you are going to get right, in the first place. Again, I support the legitimate interception of communications by official government representatives for lawful purposes. But in that sentence, there are several things that can easily go wrong. The access can be borrowed, the officials might not necessarily be that official and the lawful purpose may be questionable. Adding to that, the access might use destructive exploits, that could get stolen.

Governments have stopped trying to sell up their legitimate surveillance programs, which is wrong in my view. There should be accountability. But then surveillance is so much easier than it used to be. Anyone who has a basic IT training can use the software that is available for surveillance. Recent advances in generative AI mean that surveillance technology will become even more available soon. Security expert Bruce Schneier, mentioned in the news recently, about how AI would enable any average person to become their own intelligence agency. Using AI to summarise vast amounts of conversational data, that would have previously taken thousands of analysts, manually listening to it. All of that can be done using language models, in a fraction of the time and with very low costs. Part of the equation is access to systems, the other part is being able to process vast amounts of seemingly unrelated information, to come out with "actionable intelligence". GenAI appears to be stepping into that role. The online approach to investigations is made more attractive.

I think we also need to mention the contribution of the wrong side of human nature – as I and a few other see it. Since the fall of man, there has been a range of psychological needs in the rich and powerful, to be able to control the population and conquer their enemies. The frailty of human nature does not change, it merely modifies into different behaviours. And in selfishness, greed and lust for power, the kingpins of this world are keen on keeping everyone else in a state of vulnerability. For one reason or another. With the most recent need, of safety being computers and the internet.

Software manufacturers have a development cycle that creates software to take to market. When it is ready, the software companies like to put the product out in preview and then general availability these days. Or latest and stable release. But there are many companies who choose to build their products on software that is not classed as general availability (GA) and you cannot help but think this has something to do with human nature embedded in business conversations.

Purchasing teams and lawyers - write contracts for IT agreements. What if they included a clause that said that software had to be guaranteed secure for ten years. If there are any bugs found in their software or hardware, the supplier has to pay a reasonable penalty. So eventually greed starts to accelerate security, instead of insecurity. But taking the first step is the most difficult part. I cannot imagine any company wanting to launch into doing that unilaterally. There were some tech regulation laws issued in 2023 in the US, to do with technology contracts. Although the legal definitions are probably different. These ideas may be within the sphere of public recognition and appetite.

These are all human centric factors that are working together to prevent the general global acceptance of hackproof technologies. The main one, as mentioned is the useability factor.

What are the likely changes that will restrict IT security progress?

Depending on who you ask. There might be a number of factors influencing how we do IT security, or don't do it. A lot of IT is now done in the public cloud. The cloud service provider side of the shared responsibility model is very tightly controlled and wrapped tightly in NDAs, security audits and volumes of reassuring documentation. Overall, my experience over the past thirty years in IT, is a positive one moving to mostly cloud hosting, around seven or eight years ago. Incidents tend to be less frequent and less intensive. The numbers of hackers have greatly increased and so has their skill but at the same time the level of security hardening has also increased. Incidents have become more visible through the ransom/exposure method.

When I started in IT, I was involved in a wave of personal computer networking, that superseded decades of mainframe computing (size of a bus) and minicomputers (they were the size of a small wardrobe). Mainframe computer had engineers and computer "scientists" who wore lab coats, like doctors. It was a cult-like closely knit information society that ordinary people were not privy to. It is not too farfetched, to think of the cloud service providers as returning the world of IT, to a similar situation. Although now, the customer is able to configure up their servers (IaaS), deploy containers and webapps (PaaS) and string together reactive events and code snippets behind APIs (serverless cloud). The future will probably become a more enclosed fortress of secrecy and insider knowledge.

As artificial intelligence moves the technical bar, to a level where the customer issues Natural Language Processing (NLP) commands. Like "build me an online sales platform that allows the public to buy furniture, that is sourced from XYZ wholesalers". The AI will do all the work to build the cloud infrastructure and web application. The cloud customer does not have to have any technical staff or know how to program or manage databases. It is all done automatically by the cloud provider. That level of abstraction may sound futuristic. But it could 'actually' only be a few months away, as an invention and maybe a few years away, as a product. In reality though, my feeling is that cloud engineers, and consequently technical security engineers have a good few years left, outside of just working for a handful of large cloud providers. And spending all their time with AI bots. It sounds quite bleak and dystopian when put like that, but I am sure we will make the best of it.

But once one technical milestone has been achieved. The surge of human progress will be looking for the next thing to aim for. It would make sense that it will not necessarily be locked into the cloud provider's gift. At the moment, many of the cloud service providers are competing to find ways of accelerating the machine learning technology, by implementing machine models in silicon instead of using general purpose computation, in the form of graphical processing units. This has fallen heavy on the environmental lobby for using too much power to train large language models and then use them. A lot of the cloud providers are sourcing energy from renewable providers, to give their services a sustainable edge. But implementing in silicon, using technologies like FPGAs, or ASICs means that highly repetitive cyclical processing is instead transformed into a lightning fast one-pass calculation in silicon. It wins on two fronts. Both for its green credentials and also for performance. So, the cloud providers have been busy buying up electronics firms, to race towards being the leaders in producing the hardware models, that meet a growing customer demand.

One of the effects of moving software processes into their electronic form for use with AI, may be to better envision the way that business critical resources can be implemented in hardware. The result may be to make more secure systems. It is possible this could result, as a natural historical progression. It will undoubtedly involve all the same people, but with different hats on.

Ж

Section Introduction: IT Security Principles
What are the current conceptual principles of security – they are not tied to any technical implementation and can be universally applied to tangible and non-tangible security controls. They are the general qualities that security controls might have. These have been divided up into eight groups of principles: safekeeping, placement, cryptic, assignment, magnificent, constancy, action and lantern. When you reduce the current security activities down to their conceptual principles. Those principles have mostly been around since pre-history but in different forms.

It is also worth mentioning when we speak about IT security, what do we mean and how we convey it do have an effect on our listener but maybe do not have an effect on outcomes. The perception of security is at its heart a feeling of optimistic confidence, coupled with safety and the stillness of order. Many security officers convey these feelings in the way they do business. But recently a number of CISOs have found themselves being prosecuted for falsely conveying a sense of security, when the reality was very different.

There is a cognitive dissonance effect with the emotional and logical alignment of security. When I have attended some application discussions, the focus of the meeting is very often packed with vision, amazing new features and marketing jargon. At some point, the thought will cross my mind, "just show me the code". And I think the same thing should happen with security. We need to be clearer about the confidence the fuzzy feeling is based on.

Security feels like the warm hug of a loving parent. We should not get confused about that. It should have its rightful place.

3 THE SAFEKEEPING PRINCIPLES
trusted person, confirmed identity, physical possession, manual process, known good state, hardening, fearsome reputation

Trusted person
Examples: vetted staff member, qualified professional expert, supplier staff member under contractual delivery and management audit, security guard, HR team, company directors, supplier management team, lawyers

The concept of a trusted individual is the cornerstone for any society and that also goes for a technology environment. Philosophically, you could ask what are the dimensions of that trust, what do we trust that person or organisation for? You may not trust them to always be honest, but you might trust them to do the right thing, if someone's life is at stake. On the other hand, you may trust that they will never fail to say things that is not defensible in a court of law. But will then find some way of never quite delivering the service, that was at the root of your needs. But trust is necessary to continue to do business. The same as with traffic lights, if everyone follows the expectations and trusts one another, there are no collisions. Human trust, and perhaps in some cases faith, is a core principle in ongoing security and most other principles are dependent on it, starting with safe possession.

At some point during the early 2000s, there was a forensics promotion by the SANS Institute, based around the idea of knowing your enemy, or at least what bad looks like. We all have a bias that is wired to be cautious around people, that our inner radar considers to be hostile, or bad trouble. This varies from person to person and from generation to culture. "One man's meat is another man's poison", as the saying goes. Some people do not trust the poor, other the rich. Some are suspicious of suits and others will not do business without them. Although attribution is the most difficult part of cyber investigation. It is arguably possible to identify someone from how they operate. You can tell whether the stately home was broken into by a local teenager, or a master jewel thief. There are calling cards and tell-tale signs, or an absence of them. The trusted person generates trustworthy looking behaviours, within trustworthy systems. So, the concept of trusted person then expands into ongoing behavioural monitoring, manager interviews and possibly covert surveillance, in some cases. Depending on the risk, what industry you are in and whether they trigger alerts.

After having worked with the Met Police as an external security consultant for around seven years. Sometime later, I read in the papers that during the time I was supporting them, the force had let go around 250 people, for running vehicle licensing searches, without a valid reason. The Met had around 50,000 staff at the time. But that is still a high proportion of trusted individuals. Who had for one reason or another, decided not to stick to the rules. I was not involved in that side of data loss security but it demonstrates that the application monitoring was very sharp. Directors who manage HR performance, are generally very keen to make the point that just because you have the freedom to look up where your ex-girlfriend moved to. It does not mean that you can do it. But I was shocked at the number of people who were willing to risk it. Even though they knew they were being monitored.

There have been several organisations that have expanded the science of detecting and categorising insider threats. I remember watching a presentation at InfoSec London from a company that is now no longer around. But they had been tracking criminal gangs online and had infiltrated their attempts to coerce commercial staff members into giving them access and sending them customer databases. Some of the emails they had intercepted were outrageous, like "Hello, you don't know me but if you send me your company's customer database, we will give you ten percent of whatever we sell it for". Figures on the number of insider staff assisting attacks, vary from around 1% to 14% of attacks will include some form of insider assistance. I like to think of it that one in ten actual incidents, will include the willing co-operation of someone in the organisation. Whether they fully know what they are doing or not. Some research has been done on this subject and the Carnegie Mellon University has a research capability into insider threat actors that has some interesting past papers. I think it is fair to say that Tor browser and easier access to the dark web, has made it easier for company staff to go straight to the criminals, without the need for solicitation from the criminals.

Confirmed identity

Examples: mutual TLS certificates that prove client and server devices are who they say they are, primary forms of national identity, passport, photo driver's license, cloud resource tagging, password/passkey, fingerprint

When computer architects design a system, they use an entity diagram to describe the components of the system and how they relate to each other. An entity is just a discrete object, it could be a server, a website, a database, a firewall or gateway. In the entity diagram there are human entities and computer entities. For human entities, it is straightforward to confirm whether they are who they say there are, you just need to check their credentials, like a passport. Or in the case of authentication, checking their password, or session token. Computers also have identities when it comes to communicating within the system.

Not all interactions are human. Some computer entities will speak to other computers and the two parties need to ensure that they mutually identify each other to avoid sending confidential data to the wrong destination. You might ask, that does not make sense because they are both on the same network, how could that be? But within a network of thousands of potential endpoints, there is a very good chance that a hacker might be able to redirect their connection to themselves. Without going into the technical details, there are lots of ways to intercept and redirect network traffic. Maybe less now with the controls put in place by cloud service providers but still there are needless to say, many options.

So how do servers prevent sending data to a fake destination, how do they foil the masquerading attacker? Well, use of the IPSec VPN technology is an effective (if not often challenged) secure tunnel between two computers on a network, or between two remote networks. This is frequently used in military scenarios. Once established at a low level, data can be confidently sent the correct recipient. More recently HTTPS/TLS has been used to replace IPSec. But it does not have the same certainty in confirming identities. So using local networks has lost popularity and been replaced with public Wi-Fi and personal VPNs. Using mutual TLS to confirm both ends of the connection is an available mechanism but it is often not used. All of the ideas about system identification in the past few years have centred around X509 certificates, also known as Public Key Infrastructure (PKI), or just website padlock symbol at the top of your browser. If you click on the padlock, you can see the certificate of the website owner, that is approved by a national certificate authority. If the certificate is not signed or does not contain a signed value that states the official domain name of the website that you are visiting. Then the browser will tell you that the certificate is bad and ask whether you care. If not, you can proceed.

But that check to see if the certificate is valid was being bypassed by some gangs who were intercepting network traffic to redirect all request for social media, or banks, or company websites, to their fake website. The validation was also being redirected. So the gangs were able to impersonate the validation checks. Subsequently, the validation was pinned to the certificate, imaginatively called Certificate Pinning. This has helped to improve server identification. But certificate authority certs are being compromised frequently and before they can be removed from the laptop, criminals are selling them on the dark web for use in these interception schemes. Venafi did some interesting research into this and other companies like RecordedFuture track the behaviour of dark web actors. It is clear now that server identification is a precarious activity. Probably catching up with the market for fake passports.

Going back to the human identity, some countries seem to be making strides in improving national identification, even with the perils of personal liberty being at stake. The cat and mouse chase between criminals and national administrators, trying to avoid forgery, by applying even more elaborate forms of biometrics. Imprinting unique untraceable patterns, to make documents more authentic. Meanwhile other forms of personal identity have peaked in maturity, such as LinkedIn, which has seen incredible security value. With every identity validated through community sponsorship and long-standing connections, to other well-respected individual. Like having an instant form of business reference, backed by hundreds and thousands of common contacts. But this security value has to be offset against the open channels made available for sophisticated fraud and phishing. Last year, there was a campaign to populate LinkedIn with many fake CISO accounts, known as Sock Puppet accounts. That could be used by criminals to facilitate fraudulent correspondence. Made more convincing through linking the fake accounts and connecting to unwitting victims.

Taking a moment to think about the ways in which identities are confirmed. Since ancient times forms of biometrics have been used to confirm identity. Whether it is statuesque likeness of the ruling Emperor in his court. To the unique complexity of his signet ring, that allows sealed documents to impress the people of that time that the ruler had indeed signed the document. Fast forward to medieval artists, whose unique styles left no doubt who created the masterpiece. In more recent times methods of measuring personal human characteristics have been used to confirm identity. In the form of biometric identity.

In fact, as part of my role in security I have had to use fingerprint and retina scanning technology on several occasions. Some biometric technologies have a high level of accuracy, or Crossover Error Rate (CER) than others. Some are just convenient, in that you do not need to remember a pin, or password. It does make you feel like you are in an action movie when someone asks for a retinal scan.

I spent an interesting Saturday afternoon in my workshop once. Trying to lift my fingerprint from a glass tumbler. Using an HB pencil, some sandpaper and a paintbrush. When I could lift the fingerprint onto a piece of sticky tape, I was able to mould it into a piece of warm thermoplastic putty. Which I then cast with epoxy liquid metal. It took several attempts, but I managed to get a very impressive clear cast of my fingerprint in a conductive material. Checking first that it was the finger I used to unlock my iPhone. Then I tried for at least an hour to open the iPhone using the conductive cast of my fingerprint. It did not work and further reading about the technology behind the iPhone TouchID sensor revealed that, it actually scans the subcutaneous vein structure at a microscopic level and creates a mathematical model of the ridges and swirls. Magnifying the area through a sliver of microscopically thin Sapphire. I was suitably impressed and changed my view that the security strength of TouchID was better than I expected. I did all this, soon after a number of scientists had found a way of unlocking the iPhone using several now redundant techniques.

During my brief time at University, I had to produce a final year project and choose to do it on Keystroke Latency Authentication, as this was being developed as research by the postgraduate faculty. Keystroke Latency works by measuring the timing delay between pairs of common key sequences, called digraphs, that a typist uses frequently. Not all pairs of keys are sampled. To identify the user, it compares a range of average delays. One user might take on average 10ms between typing a letter T and a letter H. Whereas another user might take 12ms. If you select a range of distributions around the average for a number of key pairs, it creates a unique signature for each user. Using machine learning it is quite possible to positively identify a person, to a fairly high degree of accuracy, with as few as six keystrokes, on a numeric keypad. These are the sort of keypads used with swipe card entry systems, or ATM teller machines. But the same goes for computer keyboard entry.

As part of my undergraduate project, I also trialled mouse movement authentication, as a form of biometric identification and although my CER rate was pretty low. About ten years later, I saw in the news that DARPA were investing millions of dollars in a similar program. Wrong timing, I guess.

Biometric acquisition is more available than ever before, but it is an underutilised and sometimes very convenient security tool. Especially, when it is an optional extra that the user chooses to opt into. In doing so, it does not force anyone into something that they do not feel comfortable to do. Like a lot of people, I feel uncomfortable having the dimensions of my physical being and behaviour measured and compared. The ability of another to steal and use something that is so personal to me, like my own bodily curves and imprints. I threw the liquid metal mould and sticky tape in the rubbish bin, when I had finished with it.

There is another aspect to the concept of confirmed identity that I am going to describe as "substantial elaborate representation". It is the effect of confirming an identity through agreeing with social norms, to do with possessions, status and associations. Let me give an example. When I am asked to work with an unknown startup company. Sometimes I will check to see whether the company has office buildings, with their name on the front. It could be easy for a con artist to fake a company. Perhaps if they occupy fifty to a hundred seats on a third floor of an office building, it is more likely. It is not a sure-fire way of confirming identity. But it is a social norm that we use all the time to confirm that the people we do business with are genuine. Does the company have any recent news stories with pictures of the CEO with well-known figures? Are they registered with the DNB directory. Are there references to them on other website, using the Google wildcard search "link:thecompany.com" may show up well-known websites with a link to their website. Has anyone invested lots of money in them recently?

Of course, it is possible to fake all of these sorts of things in an elaborate scam. Like the guy who sold the Eifel Tower twice. But it is less likely to falsely represent them, when there are a number of hard-to-fake things associated with the company. It is amazing just how much we depend on this concept in business. Just think how hard it would be, and how creepy, if instead, to do business we had to use strong biometrics, linked to confirmed national identities. Rather than having a drink with a bloke down the pub and arranging for his nephew to come over and have a look at the boiler on Saturday. I think I would instinctively prefer the latter, even if I know as a security person the former is better. The risk drives the verification method. As any special agent movie will tell you.

Passkeys are a new entrant into the identity market. In simple terms, they link the user's identity to their device and then authorise the device, by storing a complex token string. This is then used to authenticate the device on behalf of the user, who validates themselves to their device, each time, using a fingerprint, or some other biometric. There is no need to invent complex passwords or remember them. No need to use a password manager or keep a long list of them on a piece of paper somewhere. So the approach is convenient, when compared to passwords. But I have heard several times it being described as more secure. In my opinion, passkeys is not more secure, as a mechanism. It is less accurate, as it is bound to the device instead of the user. You could argue that it is bound to the user more securely, through the biometric aspect. But it is still primarily bound to the device. Which is less secure than being bound to a secret, that is only momentarily entered and can change independently of the device, email account, mobile number, or social media ID. Passkeys could be said to be more secure because passwords have clearly failed and are now the target of most online attacks. Using decoy login pages and doing password spraying. Currently, there is considerable convenience in passkeys over passwords, as an "inconvenient and failed security control". And passkeys are seen as the better option. Passkeys authenticate the Human to the Device and the Device to the Resource. Backed by the authoritative source of identity, which might be an email account, or mobile number. Enforced through a strong access control mechanism, that prevents the keys from being stolen. Like Windows tokens are stolen using Mimikatz/Kiwi.

Physical possession and physical access controls
Examples: mobile phone in your hand, laptop in a cupboard at home,

server in a secure data center. Hardware token in a safe that no-one else has regular physical access to.

Having a computing device in your hands, on your desk, or in your server room, can be a reassuring security control. If you know that the only way of compromising the computer is to physically attach to its electronics, or local comms port. But logical access is not the same as physical access. Most access at a meaningful level, where application functionality and data are available are reached through logical access, across a network and through a login page. But physical access is the starting point for any secure system.

It is possible to lock down digital devices with hardened steel and locks. So that only a narrow user interface is available and these kiosks can sometimes be seen in places like city centres, or airports. Giving the public information about local amenities. Cashpoints (ATM teller machines) are also an example. But as we know, sometimes the cash machine will eject all its cash, given the right input. Skimming cards is also a well-known weakness. So, ensuring that your technology is in the safe possession of someone you trust.

Physical security is most effective when IT systems do not need to be connected to any networks. This is a very rare use case nowadays. Usually physical security is a baseline, accompanying a range of both physical and logical security controls. Placing too much stock in physical security is not going to help without online security and vice versa.

Manual process
Examples: filling out a paper form, printing manuals, turning a physical handle, visiting an office, unplug the cable, turn off the power

There has been a resurgence during the 2020s of retro music technologies and this year 2024, has seen vinyl record sales at the same level they were in the last century. Why do the younger generation prefer older technology? Could it be that they do not want to sit around trying to work out how the mobile app settings work. Perhaps they just want to jump about and dance instead of squinting. A just works solution is a component of good user experience design that perhaps is missing from some modern music technology.

Going back to security controls. When a ships mate is trying to board the lifeboat on a sinking ship. They will want to use a manual crank. You probably do not want to rely on the very fine-looking LCD display, whose electricity supply may have stopped working, or be on fire. In the same way, during security incidents. Having some information at hand when all the systems have gone offline, will make you the most important person in the company for a few hours, days, or weeks. Having experienced at least one major disaster recovery first hand. Having manual forms that you fill out by hand and print outs of all the most important information, like lists of telephone contacts and procedures to rebuild servers once confluence, or SharePoint have been wiped out. These are useful things to have. Why not print them off this week, put them in a folder and then update them every six months. There is no end to the jobs that need to be done but some of them need special attention.

Think of the manual telephone switchboard in the 'John Wick' films, You could put it down to cinematographic fantasy, but it makes a lot of sense, and some large organisations still rely on technology from fifty years ago, for exactly that reason. If it is not broken, don't fix it. If it means the difference between success and bankruptcy, definitely don't fix it.

Social engineering can be used to bypass manual processes. But it is hard. Take as example, a process that requires someone to visit a registered company office and speak with a security officer. Fill out a local online form, print it out and countersign it. The officer attaches a photo they have just taken. The physical paper documents are then transported by trusted hand, and stored in two separate locked filing cabinet, in two locked back-offices, in two separate secure buildings, with separate teams of guards watching them 24x7. It should not be underestimated how much effort is required to undermine this records system, compared to the 'web console click' approach. Especially if your buildings have low-cost missile protection. I worked with some colleagues once whose office was shot at with an RPG. We decided it was not infosec related.

Known good state
Examples: a newly installed server, someone who has just passed an exam, validated and signed software, antivirus and endpoint protection, code and website security scanning

This has to be one of the most broken principles in this collection. The principle is a philosophical one that says the following: "everything is orderly, as I want it to be, the state is consistent and in full control".

Now, anyone who knows about software support will know that even a modest open-source project has tens of thousands of lines of code, and they are constantly changing. Modern browsers and operating systems have millions of lines of code. With closed source development, the same is true but it is not visible to the customer, or the attackers. It is possible to scan the code. But seldom is the code fully read, understood and questioned in a way that reveals every security bug. Whether it is a vulnerability, a virus, or a backdoor.

Recently I took a web penetration testing course and the company that designed the course also produced one of the industry's leading web application security scanners. They reckoned that scans only pick up around fifty percent of security issues. With issues such as authentication implementation and business logic errors being widely missed. So the security industry is led into the false assumption that there is such as thing as known good state.

There is also the bias created by big tech marketing, that became apparent on a couple of occasions, when I was reviewing the security of some major tech companies. The review was hindered by the effects of compassionate news stories, about how a new entrant to an existing market had particular set of security issues.

Overall, the competitors in the market each had met compliance requirements for security risk management and had a good set of certifications and audit reports but under the hood, they were still all dependent on vast quantities of treacherous code and multi-use platforms. Like walking into a kitchen that appears to be clean, only to open a cupboard and find something very distasteful. The user perspective looks fine, everything works okay. But known good state is the most significant broken security principle. Moving away from it would take considerable mental effort. And it would also take considerable effort to align technology, with our positive view of it. If an operating system has received monthly security patches since it was released, in theory it has never been secure and probably never will be. We need to get over that somehow.

Hardening – including least functionality and reduced complexity

Examples: patching, designing software securely to avoid any possible vulnerabilities, applying configuration security scripts

Hardening is a principle that probably dates back to medieval warfare and stock car racing. Taking an everyday thing, whether it is a castle, or a car, or a computer system and applying measures to better resist malicious blows. With a building that might be fitting bars to the windows and steel door surrounds. With a car, that might be installing a rollbar and tough bumpers. With a computer system that might be removing anything that an attacker could target and take-over.

Hardening, as a concept makes sense with tangible objects. But it is harder to prove with computer systems. Looking at the HackerOne Hacktivity reports, you have got to ask, how much effort went into breaking in. I put this principle after Least Functionality, to make it clear that you could have only one application on a server. But without hardening, it can still be compromised. The two concepts are related but the difference is subtle. One is removing functionality, and the other is making the remaining functionality resistant to attack.

Hardening is a vague concept, but it is used very frequently in security conversations, as shorthand for a range of activities that aim to improve risk. Computer systems used in the business world are constantly under attack by very innovative hackers. Anyone who has seen how creative and masterful technologist the competitors in a CTF Capture the Flag competition are. Would know that it does not take them very long to work out how to get into applications, that they have never seen before. That there is no published vulnerabilities for. Checkout the DefCon CTF challenge videos, or PicoCTF on Github.

Businesses operate computing environments for a wide range of purposes. Take for example a data analytics and business intelligence lab. Even with a reduction in functionality, the bespoke nature and advanced, possibly untested features. Will make the system weak, in the face of a creative attacker. Like comparing a museum botany lab, full of butterflies and glass jars, to a children's play activity centre. Some environments are hardened because every process and interface will be put under duress and possibly even violence in some cases.

Contemporary data analytics systems could be handling millions of records with customer deliveries, goods received and payment data; personal information on criminals, suspects and terrorists; financial transaction and investments; control telemetry for improving power generation. All of these vital pieces of information could be available in a data analytics lab.

But the nature of the lab and how it delivers applications. What actions the analysts think are acceptable. Because in a lab analysts will be acting more like developers than normal users. There are also human processes to factor in. How transactional data moves about and how access is tracked. These are all prone to weakness and do not meet the notion of hardened in my opinion. This is a widespread issue. Throughout all the industries that use data analytics. There has been some excellent research work done by Gartner, on security monitoring for data analytics platforms. As a secondary control for the lack of opportunity to harden.

Fearsome reputation
Examples: association with violent stakeholders, private army, grandeur effect, protection racket, data recovery specialists

One of the most underrated factors in deterring criminals from attacking your systems, is the prospect of angering a collection of menacing hidden figures, lurking in the background. Who are capable of "killing you real bad", to quote Brad Pitt in the film Inglorious Basterds. To create this really takes some doing.

For most modern companies, they do not want to give their customers the impression they are somehow linked to criminal gangs, or secret society hitmen. But without letting your adversaries know that there will be a price to pay if they rob you, it is more likely to happen.

If you take a substantial amount of money away from any billionaire, you can expect that they will try to recover the money. How they do that will depend on a number of things, but we could assume they will hire private detectives to follow the clues. They will use snouts, with an ear to the criminal underworld and internet informants to get wind of who was responsible. They will then probably hire a group of hard men, or ex-military mercenaries, to capture the thieves. Once they have what they came for, they might work with the local authorities, to make sure that the criminals do not get another opportunity to rob someone else. This differs from a lot of small businesses, who do not have the means to hire private armies to do their rough work. Instead, they may just report the theft to the police and get a range of different responses, depending on local resources, availability of clues and the state of national politics.

There are a number of emerging "consultancy" provider in the data recovery space. Which is a sort of grey area. You may disagree but my understanding is that there is still a lot of blurring between hiring a lynch mob and contracting a consulting firm, who will go and get the bad guys for you. A fearsome reputation should be more of a deterrent than it is.

Take for instance the kidnapping of Freddie Heineken, the lager magnate. During the later part of the last century, a gang of Dutch workmen decided to kidnap the multi-millionaire industrialist and hold him to ransom. They got hold of the money and Freddie was released. But in the end it did not work out well for the gang. And their leader was eventually shot dead by an assassin and two of the others went to prison. The remaining criminals went on the run always looking over their shoulders. Not what they would have hoped for. They thought that getting the cash would be the hard part. They did not realise that getting away with it, over the next ten years, would be even harder.

Having spent a while doing security operations, I have been in the lead technical role, whilst finding and apprehending several groups of hackers. That sounds impressive, and it would be satisfying to say that they are all currently behind bars. But that is not the way that it works. Your average hacker is very keen not to give you useful evidence that can be used in court. And even if they are captured red handed. It very quickly appears that you are not getting anything from their equipment. But that does not mean there is no evidence available. So they are going to prison for their crime of trespassing. No, trespassing is not an imprisonable offence, on the whole. What about the Computer Misuse Act, or similar local laws. Well, actually it is hard to press a conviction and usually it is just classed as going with intent, which is less than six months in jail.

Even the most notorious hackers probably only get three years in prison at a time. I remember hearing that TJMaxx (TKMaxx in the UK) was brazenly hacked by a criminal, through their open Wi-Fi network. The hacker did not do much to cover up his unexplained wealth and soon found himself explaining it to the authorities, which saw him getting ten years in a US jail. Which is the top end for technical hackers in my experience.

But you could rationalise that a hacker is also a useful ally and can work off their debt to society in more useful ways, by being repurposed as an ethical proponent. A shift in power. So no. There were several hacking groups caught on my watch. But no prison time for anyone. It does not seem fair to me. I expended a great deal of energy. But that was not my call to make. The evidence was all there as far as I could see.

In the UK there are three basic purposes for incarceration, as I understand it - punish, reform and protect society. I cannot see how the prison system is able to provide any of these, when it comes to hackers. Maybe I could study criminality and I might change my view.

Going back a few decades, in Europe. And even today in places like Africa and India. There are criminal street gangs who will call into local shops and restaurants in the local area and tell the owner that they will offer them protection, if the owner will give them protection money, when they ask for it. People of my age will remember it happening very frequently in Western Europe during the 1970s. Protection rackets were big business in places like Chicago, USA during the 1920s. Small businesses were not able to afford to hire their own security team, or licensed bouncers. So instead, some chose to pay the local gangs, who may, or may not have provided support, based on circumstances and natural law principles. When visiting some criminal web servers, during investigations, I have come across references to gangland bosses, on the command line header of the webserver. Not something that an average user would see. But to a technical person trying to break in, it would be very clear they were about to cross a line.

What appeals to a hacker when selecting a target on the internet. Well, this is speculative. But we could assume that a lot of ransomware gangs are just picking targets at random and depending on their moral feelings at the time, they might go after hospitals, utilities, any sort of sensitive area of IT. But when it comes to some targets, they might get cold feet and decide not to go any further. For instance, online gambling websites, are renowned for being effective at cyber security. Then there are fellow criminals, in the dark web world, The obvious advanced security challenges have come from gangs that host violence and sexual exploitation sites. Also, more frequent now, drugs markets and sellers of other online criminal services. Someone choosing a target to hack, would likely think twice before trying to hack on an adversary, whose general day job is trickery, theft, or murder.

There are also hard targets in other areas. Knowing that you are likely to be deported to a shipping container in a third country, if you decide to hack into the computer systems of a national security services, is also a strong deterrent in my view. Whether that happens, might be open to discussion. I am more inclined to think that you would get many years of well-paid involuntary community service behind a keyboard. Not sure what is more of a deterrent.

Having a fearsome reputation has been around as a security principle since very early times. The Kings and Queens of England went hard on the principle during the late Middle Ages. The Tower of London was where the royals sent their enemies to rot in dark cells. If that was not scary enough, it was surrounded by a moat that contained polar bears that would eat you alive, if you tried to escape. Similar parallels with dark web services and eating people alive are likely still being used as deterrents and probably to good effect. But I am not sure this can be applied to protecting lawful businesses in the 21st Century.

4 THE PLACEMENT PRINCIPLES
enforcement point, positional advantage, dedicated use, isolation

Enforcement point, barriers and demarcation
Examples: security guard, checkpoint, firewall, locked door, auth process, libc

In security terms the enforcement point, or pinch point, is where potentially insecure items have to pass through, e.g. data, documents, connections, people. Like entering a secure facility in like a military base, you have to pass through the entry post. With guards and a barrier. You cannot just break through the fence, or you will be spotted and captured. The enforcement point is a useful idea because it gives a specific place, to bring to bear the other security controls that you might have. So, when receiving email, the mail relay might be considered the enforcement point, and it might be the ideal place to put your spam filtering. The enforcement point principle is reliant on known good state, safe possession and positional advantage.

It is also linked in some cases, to the legacy idea of full trust networks. Enforcement points are often the bridge between internal and external areas. With the perimeter as a barrier between more secure and less secure areas. In practice, this concept has declined significantly over the past twenty years with current estimates of the additional risk value of a "trusted network" of around 10% when using the NIST CVSS risk calculator (https://nvd.nist.gov). You can try it for yourself. The difference in metrics are an adjacent local network, to a multi-hop routed network (CVSS does not draw a distinction with the public internet and other large AS network). That means a critical vulnerability on the internal network might become a high-risk vulnerability on the internet.

I cannot imagine many information security managers, would be happy putting a system with a high risk vulnerability on the internet. But are often quite content to live with a high-risk vulnerability on an "internal only" restricted leg of a company network. The difficulty is that some business folks never get past the idea of firewalls as being the way into a network. They do not realise, for some reason, although it has been said enough times. That any hacker that gets a member of staff to click on the wrong link, can then pivot through that laptop, onto the rest of the company network. Essentially turning that laptop into an open firewall entry point. That means that the company has two layers of firewalls, a single remote access server but several thousand laptop pivot points. Like a big sieve. That serve as an open door into the trusted company network. The trojan malware on the laptops sends requests out to the internet, asking their zombie master's to give them the next instruction, by way of reply. Search for "Reverse Connection" on Wikipedia for more info. The recommended way to prevent this is usually a combination of Endpoint Protection (EPP) software, web filtering and using very restrictive egress filtering, in some cases.

In physical security, the perimeter fence (you understand) is usually the barrier that prevents intruders from entering. A demarcation is not a barrier but just shows you where the legal ownership boundaries begin, like a small hedge around a front garden, or those studs you sometimes see in the pavement of big cities. It tells you that you are now on someone else's patch. Gangs sometimes "tag" the boundaries of their territory with graffiti, in a similar way.

Perimeter fences may not be very effective at stopping drones from entering a campus area, but some enforcement points are still effective. Take for example the use of access gateways in the zero-trust concept. The enforcement point does not give access to a network. Instead, it gives out credentials that permit the user access to applications, using strong authentication and biometrics in most cases to tie the user to the device, to the gateway, to the account. Demarcation in computer systems is sometimes given as an "Access Prohibited" warning on a login page. This is actually more effective from a legal perspective, than a lot of other security controls.

When I first started working with cloud, I was intrigued to find out that some cloud providers allow all virtual machines open access to the internet. You have to manually setup an enforcement point and add an enterprise firewall, if you need one. This was quite disconcerting from a security point of view. I assumed by default the cloud VM service would deny all traffic out by default, like some other clouds do. But from a user flexibility point of view, you are up and running straight away, without any need to know anything about firewalls or routing. If you were concerned about security as cloud customer, I suppose you would fix the issue. It is straightforward to fix. So, this is a customer choice.

Positional advantage
Examples: internal company networks, air-gapped networks, radio distance, line-of-sight

Another legacy principle but one that still may have some value, is positional advantage. This could be standing in a geographical position, connecting to a local physical network, having access to a building. It could be standing in front of a terminal in a data centre. In some cases, the advantage could be from visiting a foreign country, that has a national firewall. Although all of these seeming advantages add value, they really should not be considered to have the same security value that they had, before the massive rise in the numbers of hackers occurred, during the past twenty years.

Most professional hackers have some kind of skill in social engineering and the knowledge of how to successfully walk into a building. Some hackers will use the USB key drop technique to get malware onto the desktop of an unsuspecting employee. Who happened to find their flash drive, just lying on the ground, in the car park. The BadUSB approach was widely popularised in 2014 with the work of Karsten Knoll and is currently perpetuated for pen testers by Hak5 amongst others. Even now, the first go-to control for top security systems, is the air-gapped network. This means that none of the computers in the local wired network have a gateway to access the internet.

When I first started in IT in 1992, this was the way in which all company networks were operated. There was no worldwide web. Although the internet existed, it was mainly for academics and allowed basic email. Most companies did not use it. They would communicate on internal wide area communications between cities over private leased circuits and use client-server computer systems. Using legacy Ethernet protocols, as there were no websites or TCP/IP generally before that time. If you wanted to hack a company, you had to go into their buildings. There was not even Wi-Fi, that would allow someone to hack from the local vicinity. No, the attacker had to go into the building, or find a way of tapping into wide area comms cables, running underground, or through conduits.

In the past ten years, the only air-gapped networks have been for things like military, defence contracting and extreme forms of scientific research. I could be wrong but I think that is the limit of it. But even one workstation with a USB Wi-Fi dongle is enough to let a hacker in. In the 1990s, some state sponsored attackers were so desperate that they invented the TEMPEST attack, which used electro-magnetic emanations from early computer monitors captured using a directional antenna, to remotely view what was showing on the monitor of someone in the building. The images were shaky and blurred. It must have been a relief when finally, the internet gave them a more comfortable place to spy from, than a cold damp transit van outside on the street. Fortunately, recent monitors do not leak in the same way. But there have been some other attacks that leak information from air-gapped networks, like the "Mosquito" attack that uses speaker and microphone of two compromised devices, one with internet access and another without. There is also a novel new mobile phone gyroscope technique. Whose novelty is on a parr with the mobile phone "Invisible Finger" attack. All good fun and no bullets required.

Within some large companies, there is still usually a few sub-networks, isolated from the main user network. That are used to host important systems. Network isolation has for a long time been promoted as a way of protecting database back-ends. But in more recent years, the database has become less protected, as it used to be. There are many cases where databases have been compromised en-masse, in publicised attacks. As they have been poorly positioned on exposed networks.

User networks, where you plug in your laptop, or connect your mobile phone, do not have to be completely open areas, sometimes called flat networks. Going back twenty years, most big corporations would have networks that allowed you to login to a server, on the other side of the world, if you had the right firewall permissions. With a securely configured LAN, each node on the user network can have its own unique subnet, that can only connect to a select number of filtered servers. Users are not able to communicate with other users on the network directly. This takes a lot of engineering effort and more recently where there are internal company networks, they have reverted to being more open than previously. Which says something about the expectation of security and the efforts to try to maintain it through network controls. It takes a lot of effort to maintain private company networks. Software Defined Networking (SDN) has helped somewhat to make this easier. But tough positioning constraints, have now meant that most users want the freedom to put their laptop, tablet or company mobile, directly onto the internet. Through a local Wi-Fi access point, like they do with their personal devices.

During the early 2000s, there was a movement by the Jericho Forum that called for de-perimeterisation but it did not have an immediate widespread effect. Although it was a good effort, it was not enough to change IT industry's dependence on walled garden approach to corporate networks.

Recently companies and tech providers have been promoting the idea of 'zero trust' as a replacement for company internal networks. What in-fact appears to be happening is the increased uptake of third-party SaaS vendor services and federated access providers. This is not quite the same as the original promotion of the idea. But there is a demand for greater internet freedom in companies.

Google was maybe the first company to go all out for zero-trust, following the release of a technical paper. That led to the company to a new form of access mechanism and their approach to access they named BeyondCorp. Where there is no such thing as internal and everything is out there on the internet. It is working really well for them and there are many other companies who would be keen to follow suit. From a conceptual point of view, I am not keen on the phrasing of zero trust. I think we need more of the right kind of trust, not less. But time will tell what happens with "zero trust" implementations. Hopefully they will continue to grow. Zero trust really boils down to a single internet enforcement point

The placement principles

+ strong authentication and all the other principles that support those two things, like device trust, device inventory and the trust inferer. Positional advantage also means that if you stand in the right place at the right time, you get to see the sun through the trees. Which is also nice.

Position has sometimes been used to exclude bad things, either within, or without. For example, with a prison, or jail. The inmates of a jail are the bad that is kept inside to protect the freedom of those in the outside world. On the other hand a castle was used until the end of the middle ages to keep bad out. The equivalent can be seen with IT system that use a jail or sandbox, such as a chroot jail, or browser sandbox. This is designed to contain anything bad within online content when handled by the system. The equivalent of the castle is probably the perimeterised network, keeping bad outside. But as we know, that is not a useful analogy anymore.

When the internet first came out, the proposition that everyone was talking about what to host websites in your own home and allow others to access them. After only a short time of people doing that. It became clear that there were a whole set of benefits, with using hosted data centres instead. Home hosting depended on having a fixed IP address, cool server cabinet and always-on internet. Whereas most networking was dial-up modem. That you connected, checked your email and then disconnected. You were charged per minute, like a phone call. Consumer ISPs started to issue dynamic IP addresses and although DynDNS and other services allowed home hosting to continue. It did not take off at the rate that was expected and instead everyone started to host with hosting provider services. This had the effect of centralising control and relinquishing physical possession over servers and positioning of the internet became less personal. I have not thought about that for a while.

Radio can have a positional effect. When you install a commercial Wi-Fi system, companies are wise to avoid WPA and go for ENTERPRISE Wi-Fi standards, such as EAP-TLS or EAP-LEAP instead. But the actual positioning and type of antenna can also produce a dramatic effect, in preventing intrusion from outside the perimeter of the offices. From the canteen, or one of the meeting rooms perhaps. Using a horn profiled directional antenna that point inwards and down into the room can prevent bystanders outside from hacking into your Wi-Fi network. In the past I have known some security researchers, and radio enthusiast who do all their work underground. Just to prevent the unfortunate loss of control over radio waves.

All goes to show, if you want to get there, I wouldn't start from here.

Dedicated use
Examples: any server that should only be used for one purpose (i.e., web server, database, file server), a dedicated work laptop, staff only rest rooms, building control appliances, factory logic controller

Markets tend to compete on particular features, that could be price, support, luxury, or range of other features. Tech companies have been competing on big feature ranges for a long time. This has led to what should have been a single use equipment performing processes that are not central to its purpose. Like a hammer, with a built-in screwdriver.

Many servers that should only be used for highly sensitive use, are also aggregating streaming data for other devices on the network or have a default set of secondary applications that need to be disabled. Like scripting engines and file servers. The prevalence of intelligence-based marketing means that many confidential computers, send vast amounts of usage telemetry and it seems impossible to disable this. As it's a design feature of the product and gets agreed in the purchase contract.

But multiple use does not just sit with the user interface and high-level functions. It is also a feature at the lowest level within the electronics of the device.

Since the 1970s and earlier, the development of computers, has ensured that most computers are multipurpose and can run arbitrary code. As long as a new program follows the instructions set, it will usually run. This is a necessary alignment, otherwise programming would become even more difficult than it already is. Code signing and application allowlists (like AppArmor and AppLocker) were introduced to try to restrict computers to only run authorised programs. In some cases, single use digital products have been available, some early networking devices used a very narrowly scoped rom-logic and were considered 'appliances' instead of computers. In the consumer space, the Nintendo Gameboy took fixed cartridges that contained a single program to run with an executable program written to a microSD card inside the cartridge. Although the processor could still run more than one process or thread, the early Gameboy did not have any Wi-Fi electronics and there was only one way to introduce code to run, through the solid-state game cartridge. This restricted the unit to single point use but gave the user modular flexibility through owning multiple cartridges.

Multiprocessors and multi-use computers have been fundamental to the development of computers and also means that reuse of devices, lessens the impact of disposable electronics. Where some devices may have only served their purposes for a few months. It is speculative and there may be some research showing that the average length of time an average teenager owns a mobile phone is less than a year. After which they are disposed of. Most companies plan to keep self-hosted computers, such as laptops for around three years, as a depreciated asset. This is written into most undergraduate textbooks. The laptops are then sent for recycling. This book is being typed into somebody's recycled company laptop that I bought on eBay. It is still very useful and could probably have been used for more than ten years.

Who wants to use a ten-year-old laptop. With Moore's law, meaning that the latest code volume will not run on it. Cloud data centres offer a promise of better environmental stewardship through sustainable use and offering lower tier alternatives for less mission-critical applications. AWS are still offering older and slower mechanical hard drives, instead of solid-state drives, still recently.

Throwing away single use computer hardware is a waste and there are many electronics recycling companies that struggle to make an impact in the constant flow of unused devices. The main issue as I understand it is the complex integration of precious and volatile substances, as well as plastic furnishings. That must be extracted before the metal can be smelted and turned into something else. I have watched a few YouTube videos, where amateurs try to recover precious metals from circuit boards that are no longer usable. And being very pleased with themselves, when they find a microscopic grain of gold, or silver in the palm of their hand. But it needs to be scaled up to be effective. There are moves in the global south, to process plastics into building materials, like bricks and girders by cutting the plastics into strips and congealing them with acetone or other chemicals into moulds. The cost performance is barely marginal, and the effort is considerable but it makes a difference to lock plastic into building houses that may last a few hundred years, like giant plastic children's toy blocks. It is a much healthier way of disposing of computers than choking turtles.

But overall, things might have been considerably different with the amount of waste produced, if the multiprocessor issues were identified and patched at the start. Imagine the vulnerability bulletin:

CVE-1970-0001 Multiprocessor Allows Arbitrary Code Execution. Risk: Critical. Affected Devices: All

Isolation

The placement principles

Examples: air-gapped networks, separate tenant for each customer, database in a separate private subnet, private/public resources

Isolation in terms of security could be a misnomer. Certainly, in subjective physical terms, nothing exists in complete isolation from everything else. There are supply chains, cleaners, updates, exceptional circumstances like fire alarms. All of which means that the perfectly separated IT system still revolves around things like decorators and heating systems. Local council changes to drainage and staff shortages. But for the sake of simplicity, let's start by saying that an isolated system does not have a general unauthorised network thoroughfare. It is like an "enclosed fountain" that only one should have access to.

For a long time, it was considered to be a major step forward in security, if you could isolate the local network from the internet. This focused the attention of any attackers into the local physical domain. They would need to physically travel to your local area and somehow plugin to the network. Over the years, there has been an increased dependency on having an internet connection.

A lot of software needs to be connected to the internet to validate its licensing, receive updates, send analytics, etc. This has caused security teams countless headaches, with their perfect plan of a hermetically sealed idyll. Usually, some halfway house is reached. Where the monitoring and updates are made from a management network, that is allowed access into the isolated Local Area Network (LAN). Which then means it is not completed isolated anymore. But in the minds of those who have got used to it being isolated, they may not know or care about that.

Another aspect of system design that has changed over twenty years, is the use of dedicated hardware, hosted by suppliers. Who provide an instance of their online service, just for your company. With your own server and database in their data centre. The aim being that anyone working at another organisation, who wants to hack all the other customers of that supplier, may not be able to hop over, if they discover a logical authorization bypass. In practice though, having your own server and database, costs significantly more money. It also probably does not make the solution that much more secure. It can lead to some extensive debates. "Security Theatre" is a phrase coined by security expert Bruce Schneier, that came to mind when thinking about conversations I have had about dedicated servers.

All meaning that fewer suppliers are willing to offer this kind of service anymore. And large enterprise SaaS providers, now treat every user account as if it were a fortress. Whilst exposing the SaaS application to the internet. Any user that finds a way of bypassing their own account restrictions and gains permissions to access another account has hit the jackpot. The main SaaS type that comes to mind is social media applications. But there are other applications that I can think of that have offered dedicated hardware to their customers that are now multi-tenant only. Meaning that all the organisations and users are using the same physical IT equipment. It has spurred increased attention in other areas of security prevention.

Databases are a structured way of storing data, to organise things and provide quick access. Who would need to get access to a database. In theory, only the front-end application, that all the users login to, should need to get access to the back-end database. This makes the database isolated from everything apart from the application, in an adjacent subnet. But the widespread sharing of data among many applications and possibly data privacy regulations. Have led to databases being hosted in an internet facing position, usually behind an authenticated API mechanism. The API is a simple application logic that takes an authorised request and returns values in the database, based on the parameters in the request. It is a little more complicated than that, but it is not far off having the database facing the public internet. Is this a more secure situation. Yes, in some ways it is.

Take for instance the local impresario piano player, who plays in the local village hall every Spring. Everyone thinks he is the best player in the world. Until he goes out to play concert halls and finds himself on the world stage. Hosting systems on the internet takes a lot of courage and careful planning these days. It is a tough world out there and a system whose security was robust within a local isolated network may not fare so well when exposed to the internet. In the finance industry, there has been a sevenfold increase in the number of attacks against application APIs in the past five years. And this could be attributed to financial companies moving isolated systems and putting them on the internet.

An API is a bit like a website and your browser, or mobile app can connect to it. It can be made to speak a number of computer data transport languages, like JSON, XML, or GraphQL. These transmit the website data, to your browser or app, in the background, when the webpage in your browser requests it. More importantly, APIs can also transmit data between servers, or between a database and a server, without any human intervention. This can be done when the application on the server needs some data, or some processing that is done on another server.

APIs when using strong access control mechanism like OAuth v2.0, is definitely a better solution than using a static database username and password and putting the database management interface onto the internet. For a long time, web applications, have stored database credentials on the application server, in a plaintext file. If you then put the database management interface on the internet. It would certainly be attacked almost instantly. Adding the API layer in front of the database and using strong access controls, reduces this and effectively provides a form of logical isolation. It also means that the database admin username and password, that rarely change, are less likely to get stolen and replayed indefinitely until the password is changed again. This shuts down a lot of attacks. The API restricts the type and number of process operations available to be requested. It does not have the same range of functionality as a full database management interface. But APIs are also become the target of a lot more attacks and some consider it the number one threat against finance IT.

An idea that has changed dramatically in the minds of IT people of the past ten years, is the concept of private and public resources. If you were to go back to the 1990s, when you talked about private resources, you would mean either an air-gapped network with no access to the internet. Or you would mean a resource that was only available from the company offices. You could not get to it from outside of the offices, except maybe over remote dial-in VPN. But now the meaning of private has changed to mean that the IT resource, usually a website, or API, is available on the internet because everything is, right! But the resource can only be accessed using strong authentication. That is private.

So, the meaning has changed in terms of physical isolation. Now, if something is considered public, it does not require any authentication. Like visiting a website that does not need a login and you just download the page content, or images. There has been a lot of thought leadership on this by the cloud service providers, who are keen to define public cloud and private cloud, in terms of logical isolation. Although some cloud providers will bring a public cloud cabinet into your data centre, if you pay for it. A lot of IT people are still getting used to this change in the public/private definition.

For a long time, there was a reassurance in knowing "the data is in the office" and feelings of control and being able to sleep well. Then online services started to create an appealing prospect of having data at your fingertips, from anywhere in the world, at any time of the day. All private of course, because you need to login, see. But anything risky would have to be physically isolated from the internet. Leading to the following scenario.

You would still have to go into the office, if you wanted to get access to the HR, or sales figures, or fund some private equity. You would have a list of twenty, or thirty people who had local access, they are all trusted people who you know well. You could even call them friends. The code was developed in house by another couple of colleagues. They were not the best coders, but they were trusted. But then there were some complicated security issues and in-house development needed to be partly outsourced. Now you have potentially hundreds of support staff with access to your system in another continent, they speak a different language and do not know them personally. The code they build is more complex than before and your developers are struggling to understand how it works. Some of the managers are asking to get remote access and the outsourcers have suggested a web console, instead of remote VPN because it will be quicker and more convenient. The vendor has a fully managed SaaS platform. So now your data is all on the internet.

And so the story goes on, and on. This has been the prevalence of IT progress, over the past twenty years. It has made systems more accessible but consequently, giving the impression of being less secure. Within the world of human ideas and in some cases, in reality

5 THE CRYPTIC PRINCIPLES
obscurity, applied complexity, mathematical certainty, intrigue and trickery

Obscurity
Examples: key under the door mat, server listening on a high order UDP port number that is not publicised, a secret security operations (SyOps) process, codenames

Security by obscurity used to be seen as no security at all. But in recent years, there have been real world evidence that the obstacle of obscure details does make a difference in hindering attacks. I think the point that previously led to "security by obscurity is no security" was because it became a single point of failure and was not included in a layered defences approach.

Although I was not around in the 1950s and early 1960s. This saying about obscurity may have come about for the same reason that we now talk about zero-trust in reference to perimeterized networks. If a security operation is only made up of obscurity and quirky contact arrangements, codenames and keywords.

It is understandable that the security personnel during that period would want to stop relying on obscurity, in favour of more substantial security controls. But now we have a lot of those controls available, I think there is a place for additional obscurity. Even until recently, large organisations would rotate their networking address scheme every few years. If that is not a form of obscurity, I don't know what is.

Militaries around the world rely on the use of codenames, codewords and internal references for things, in order to remain undetected and maintain secrecy. Obscurity is a major part of that subculture. The British World War II soldiers involved in "The Great Escape", named their three tunnels "Tom", "Dick" and "Harry". To ensure that they could talk about their escape plans without the guards knowing, that they were referring to codenames and not the names of actual men.

Applied complexity and exhaustable effort
Examples: encryption, transactions that rely on numerous complex parameters to be correct, complex identifiers such as the UUID standard, probability of guessing a password takes more processor iterations than molecules in the universe

In ancient times, brave warriors went out to fight in open combat. Like grown men running at each other with machetes in a field. The films portray it with backing music and aerial photography. But in reality, on the ground it would have been a scrap with lots of nasty amputations and gashes. I would imagine that the retreating wounded would have been asking themselves, why did they ever agree to it. But at least in the field of open combat you know what to expect. But occasionally, there are stories of heroes being challenged on the cerebral level, such as Theseus and the Minotaur who had to find his way through a complex maze. When faced with many doors, which one do you choose. One is an endless circle in deep darkness. Another is a brutal foe. Fast forward to the 2020s and we have encryption technology, the application of maths and structured confusion, to ensure that an attacker will never find what they are looking for. That is the idea anyhow.

There are lots of possibilities for protecting information with encryption systems. But most of the cryptography applied to data nowadays uses 'decrypt on download'. The encryption does not protect the data in any real sense. It has some value but with an authenticated session, the data is available to anyone who has the credentials, or a session token, to access the online application. The encryption is transparent in that sense.

Of course, if you went to the data centre with a small army and took the disks from the rack, you might have some luck with finding the data and then you would be faced with the challenge of decrypting it. So, it does have some value. That is actually the value of most 'encrypt on download' schemes. The only thing it prevents is physical theft. With most cloud services, the racks are fitted with break-glass technology that will destroy the data on the disk, if it is removed from the rack. There is no point in additional encryption. But in all of our compliance regulatory checks, there is always the check box for encryption. Law makers may will also ask whether the data is encrypted. As if they know that the encryption control is effective somehow. Mostly it is not.

Now in some cases it is. Take for instance the use of Hardware Security Modules (HSM), which is something like a shining jewel in a glass cabinet behind three-inch glass. Actually, it is a rack mounted mild steel box, but analogy makes it more interesting. The cryptographic keys (long numbers) in the HSM are never seen by any human. With most banks and military, they are generated in a crypto ceremony once a year. Something I had to facilitate once. That is usually attended by the IT manager, a senior exec and the security engineer (me). Some complex values are entered, and entropy introduced. The HSM is then ready to dispense and validate encryption keys for anyone who needs them. Of course, then the HSM becomes a single point of failure for any use of data that relies on it. So, you probably want more than one. And at several thousand dollars, they had better make a difference. Reading the manual first is really very important, if you are running a war, or a finance company.

With an HSM you can control who has continuing access to data. If the "encrypted" data is being used by a third-party company and you suddenly do not want to them to have access anymore, you can simply revoke the last key that you gave them, prevent them from requesting any more decryption and they no longer have access to the "encrypted" data. But if they have already decrypted the data and then you cannot see what they have done with it, they may have copied it off somewhere. In which case, there is no point to revoking their keys, they already have the data.

In another use case, probably the only one that is really effective. Your trusted staff process some file data, in trusted applications, that use the HSM to encrypt the files. You then send the encrypted files to a third-party file storage site. The third-party never see the keys, they cannot access the data to process it, so the data is secure. There are not many use cases like this. When you give data to a third-party it is usually to process it. So again, this is limited in value.

If you have an internal database and an application that stores data on it. You could use your HSM service, or if you cannot afford the full-service delivery package, the cloud equivalent managed service, such as AWS KMS. To encrypt the data with what are known as "customer managed keys". But the application just requests the keys, and the key service gives it the keys. So, the hacker has control of the application server and requests the keys and the key service gives the hacker the keys.

In practice, there may be some value in this scenario for revoking the keys once a breach has been detected. But once the data is gone, it is gone. "Decrypt on download" is the issue and there are not any easy ways around it with the current thinking about how application processes work. As I said, the most effective use seems to be in object storage.

Another use of complexity is the storage of passwords in

a database using hashing and salts. Passwords are stored in a special database, so please don't store passwords in a normal database! The access control database, usually an ESE database in a high percentage of cases, is limited to local use by the access control mechanism processes. These are hardened processes with limited user access. Passwords are hashed using a hashing algorithm that cannot be reversed. It is logically impossible, once you transform from A → B to go backwards from B back to A. When you take A, which can be any length of data. But it will be transformed into a fixed length string (usually 128 or 256 bits long) that represents the data that was entered. Small changes to the data will create completely different hash strings. It is possible to use a wordlist and guess from A → B lots of times, until you match the hash. That is where salt values come into their own.

A salt value (usually four bytes) is stored with the password in plaintext and is added to the hashed value as it goes through multiple rounds of hashing. The process of using one-time salt values and multiple rounds of hashing, is to make the use of rainbow tables difficult. A rainbow table is a pre-computed list of all the passwords and their hashes in a alphabetic sequence, it can be terabytes in size and with the use of cloud GPU systems, makes cracking a stolen user password list, much less computationally difficult.

But why you might ask would anyone want to crack a list of user passwords when they already have access to the crown jewels, that is root on the target application. Surely if they are able to obtain the list of passwords, they have some sort of full control over the system. In a lot of business applications, this is the case. There is not much else that can be achieved. But for mass market consumer applications, let's say it is called Xmail, or some other social media service. The attacker does not want to control the whole of Xmail, they just want to get access to a political leader's personal email account. The Xmail team are likely to regain control of their servers within a few days. In that case, cracking specific user passwords will get you casual access to the email account, until the politician works out that someone else has gained access and changes their password. If the hacker triggers an alert in the consumer application, the Xmail team may publicise that the user password list has been stolen. But it is possible that no one will change their passwords in response. Including the account owned by the political leader, that was the actual target of the whole breach of public security. This scenario is fictional and just for illustrative purposes.

Going back to encryption briefly, there are currently moves to start using Fully Homomorphic Encryption (FHE), which allows data to be encrypted and stay encrypted whilst being stored with a third-party. It is possible, although limited, to perform calculations and even database searches using the data that still remains encrypted. Limited studies have shown it to work but there are performance issues and a lot of improvement is necessary to arrive at a mass market workable solution.

Personally, I can see it restoring some confidence but the mathematics loses a lot of engineers, who may not be able to apply and debug issues. The libraries used to support it will probably become black boxes. This is starkly different from the AES standard, which is visible to all, and a straightforward data transformation process, if you care to dig into it. FHE, on the other hand has the same opaqueness as the inner workings of machine learning models. I can see how the code implementation works and although I studied mathematics at degree level, I had to give up and trust that other mathematician would probably agree with them.

Mathematical certainty
Examples: Diffie Helmann/RSA logarithmic non-reversable algorithm used in public key cryptography and HTTPS connections

As I explained at the start of chapter 2, when a browser, or other applications want to establish a point-to-point connection to a webserver. It uses asymmetric cryptography to exchange encryption details. This is known as in the context of company websites as Public Key Infrastructure (PKI). It is possible to share a public key (encrypting key) with some third party, who then encrypts data using the public key. That data can only be decrypted by their private key, when the third party sends the encrypted data back to them. The whole scheme depends on a piece of mathematics that if I remember, is called the discrete logarithmic problem. When values are transformed from A to B using the mathematics, it is not possible to transform back again, when only knowing what it was transformed into (this is not the same as the hash transform mentioned in the last section). But mathematics is a progressive field, and it is assumed that one day there will be a breakthrough and it will be possible mathematically to go from B back to A. When that happens nearly all of the currently used public (asymmetric) cryptography will become obsolete, as it will not offer any sort of protection. Any undergraduate mathematics student will be able to intercept and read website HTTPS/TLS connections. Even if they are using the latest software.

Mathematical certainty can be a very reassuring thing. Take for instance the recent breakthroughs in Quantum ready algorithms, such as Kyber CRYSTALS. Although the basis for things like Quantum computing and AI rest not on mathematics but on computer engineering design. The solution to meeting the threat of Quantum computing being able to calculate exponentially difficult to guess encryption values, went to a new form of encryption algorithm. Based on mathematics and not purely a complex computing process.

Mathematics appears to be used for other things in modern cyber solutions. Whereas in fact it is not maths behind the values but a computing process. This process transforms values by substituting one value for another (s-box) and transforming or rotating sets of figures (p-box). So one set of binary or text data goes into the subroutine and out pops a long fixed length number. This is not mathematics; it is a computer memory manipulation process. There are some mathematics done in some small cases but overall, the world of cryptography does not rely on mathematics but processing. It is possible to use mathematics though to prove that hashing algorithms like MD5 can experience collisions, where two files can have the same MD5 value. This was not meant to be possible, but it can be proven by mathematics, so it is a certainty.

Other uses of pure mathematics in security is the use of Kohonen self-ordering maps, used as machine learning classifiers, in data loss prevention filters. A set of documents is fed into the network. Although the process is computer based, it is the result of advanced mathematics built into the process that ensures that the documents can be neatly separated and grouped into similar types. So confidential data is separated into one pile, useless marketing brochures in another.

There is far more scope for mathematical certainty in computer design around security and I discuss this again in chapter 12. Thinking about the discrete logarithm use. One little piece of mathematical certainty has been holding the global world wide web together for twenty-five years. I think we could have more of that, in other areas of security.

Intrigue and trickery
Examples: social engineering, phishing, honeypots, hidden cameras, deception technology

One of the main strengths of the hacker proposition, is their ability to be able to hide their identity. Without this one feature of the hacker's arsenal, I would hazard to guess that they would not have much success. I could be wrong. When opening a discussion about trickery and hackers I guess it would be polite to mention the likes of Kevin Mitnick and Chris Hadnagy. Both of whom have furthered the science and practice of social engineering in the public space. Revealing some of the antics that have been going on in the world of confidence tricksters, master criminals and secret agents. The ability to be able to trick people into giving you what you want, by bending and leveraging the expected social norms, human perceptions and exploiting way in which people's minds work. This has been taken to an extreme with the invention of techniques such as Neural Linguistic Programming (NLP), that targets trigger words and other psychological features, to do mind hacking. Whenever companies commission a physical security pen test, that involves some sort of social engineering, it is good practice to establish some common sense ground rules, to avoid putting unreasonable psychological pressure on staff.

In recent years, phishing has become one of the main deliver mechanisms for social engineering attacks and a considerable number of recent phishing campaigns have not used malware links or payloads. But instead rely on staff doing things because the hacker has manipulated them into doing it. New AI tools have allowed hackers to author social engineering emails at greater scale. Overcoming previous constraints on things like language, grammar and personalising attacks using stolen data to fill in the blanks. Imagine the difference in effect, if the incoming email knows everything about your world and sounds plausible and does not make any spelling mistakes, in any one of fifteen languages. Unique emails are sent to five thousand executives. That could be a very effective phishing campaign and it is the sort of thing that is now being seen around the world.

Just a thought, but what if the defenders started phishing and social engineering the attackers? You must have seen the videos where someone takes on the cold caller, who is trying to scam them. Fairly sure this could be considered self-defence in some jurisdictions. I have never done it, but I have seen it done online a few times. I would not recommend it though.

Honeypots, if you did not know are computers that are hosted on a network, or the internet, purely for the purpose of observing what a hacker is up to. If you host a honeypot on the internet, it will only be a matter of minutes or a few hours before someone starts hacking it. You can see some of the latest techniques and exploits. It has a side windows type of software harness, that allows you to view the hacker actions without undermining the whole platform. You could reverse engineer some of the remote access malware for scientific curiosity. Security researchers have been known to use this sort of approach to discover the use of new vulnerabilities and malware types.

Honeypots should fall into the category of trickery; the point is to lure the attacker into believing they will get some sort of real-world result from their efforts. Although once I was helping a colleague prototype a Nepenthes low interaction honeypot for a client. As part of the process, I thought it only logical to scan the network, to see how it presented itself. Only to be told by NMAP that it was in fact a honeypot. No misconceptions there. Realistically, a honeypot is only as good as it is, at presenting itself as a normal looking server. Once the hacker has compromised a vulnerable listening service, they might try to test whether it is a honeypot in several ways.

Other campaigns use social media and what are known as sock-puppet identities. Like a ventriloquist with a sock on each hand talking to each other. The online identities are created to look like real people. Sometimes using face-merge filter, that creates composite facial photos of people who never existed. This approach only has limited success, depending on how thorough the attackers are at doing their homework. In most cases, even more than a cursory check would reveal that the identity was a fake. But hackers are just human and make mistakes too, you know.

Deception technology is a category of commercial software that came out of the work of honeypot enthusiasts. It creates a virtual world-inside-a-world, within large company networks, where the attacker loses perspective and may not realise, they have been sucked into a trap. Where everything is fake, and all their actions are being observed and possibly used against them. In theory that is the idea. But in practice, I have not heard about many arrests from this type of approach.

Most of the IT security technology is geared up for point response (whack-a-mole), disarming the attack in progress and then finding a way of stopping the gap, by patching the vulnerability. Deception technologies allude to another prospect. That it is possible to turn around the deception and make the hunter the hunted. To assert the upper hand.

But elaborate schemes are not always necessary to come up with a result. It is possible to arrange things carefully, so that any disturbance is noticeable. When I was a child, I read about how spies used to operate and we tried out some of the techniques around the house. So, when I went out of my bedroom, I used to tape a hair fastened between a door and a door frame. If someone came into my room while I was away, I could tell. Another technique was to leave a small amount of talcum powder sprinkled on the floor that someone might tread on and leave a mark. These are all childish examples but everyone makes mistakes sometimes, is not an unhealthy way to think about it. Hackers may be excellent at what they do, some even elite. But none of them are infallible.

But a word of warning. If you catch a bear, or a wolf in a trap. You had better be prepared to deal with it in the proper way. I would stick to shadowing someone else's research, unless you are feeling very confident.

One trick that I put together, that had some results, and no one else seemed to be doing it at the time, was to track network TTL figures. In a large corporate network, you will generally find one or maybe more routed Autonomous Systems (AS). The internet is made up of Internet Service Provider (ISP) networks that are interconnected with government, academic and other networks. All these networks have AS numbers, and you can look them up if you are interested. The AS networks interconnect together with Border Gateway Protocol (BGP), that allows network packets to be sent to the right destination. Within each corporate AS, there is usually a routing protocol like OSPF, that handles local routing of IP traffic. Each time of the network packets goes through a router, the Time-To-Live counter is reduced. TTL is used to time-out any packets that start going into a loop, otherwise they would eventually flood the network. Any traffic from a long way away will have a low TTL, because it has crossed lots of routers. Local traffic will have a high TTL and lots of hops left in its timer. By spotting the low TTL packets, you can detect rogue switches and network hacks in large networks. Only a handful of colleagues knew about this when I first started using it and there was quite a bit of action, over even such a small and seemingly insignificant trap. There are many others like it, which may not currently be used to catch out the criminals. If you are in security operations, why not do some research and invent your own.

Honeytokens is a technique similar to honeypots. The desktop support team creates some fake user credentials or session tokens, these are the honeytokens. They are injected into the computer's memory using PowerShell, or some other technique. I have written PowerShell to do this and it is fairly straightforward and works. Although the user credentials are not real, they do have a corresponding website address that is waiting to receive login attempts. When a hacker steals the credentials from the RAM of the victim computer and tries to use them. They not only reveal that they have accessed one of the company computers, but they also reveal the computer that was compromised, if each set of honeytokens is unique to the device it was stored on. This is a powerful technique.

There are also honeytokens that can be embedded into your confidential documents, along with benign malware exploits. The malware only makes a light-touch call to home, using DNS for instance. If you get the network ping, it lets you know if your confidential documents were stolen. It will also tell you the network address, where the document was last viewed from. The temptation is to include a backdoor and start hacking back at the criminals. But there may be other victims involved and randomly hacking back may not solve any problems. This is an ethical dilemma.

In the physical world, the incredible popularity of CCTV has surpassed the childhood imaginings of spies and secret cameras. Now everybody has a mobile camera, and everything is fitted with a microphone, or camera. It is surprising how anything goes amiss. But it is not the pervasiveness of cameras but the democratisation of ownership and motive that is challenging the forces of order in the world. And with deep-fake technologies like Face Swap becoming ever more accessible. It is hard to know how great the level of injustices will become. If we do not realise quickly when a security control is no longer acting in our favour.

Magic tricks are a public form of deception that have charmed people for centuries. The ability to conjure something out of nothing, in the minds of others, is a great skill to have. I remember a long time ago working with a colleague who was a member of the magic circle and also a senior security professional. I remember asking him about whether he thought there was any cross-over value between the two disciplines, and it is obvious from a defender's perspective. As well as understanding how the latest attacks work and which of the technologies you use are vulnerable. Having a general mindset that is capable of overturning and creating tactical advantages is valuable. And also good for children's parties.

6 THE ASSIGNMENT PRINCIPLES
roles and least privilege, authorized action, separation of duties, session fixation

Roles and Least privilege
Examples: permissions groups, permissions tourists, concentration risk, remote access

The concepts around access controls have come out of an alignment with company job roles. When an employee starts with a company, or government organisation, they are issued with access based on what they do for a job. So everyone that works in the building would have general access to the building. When they sit down at any computer in main building, they should be able to login with their general user access and see their applications and documents. This is the received expectation of employees in millions of companies over the past thirty years. Someone working in the finance department would probably have additional access to the finance systems, if they are involved with payments, they might additionally have access to the organisations banking applications and card readers. This might need to be done in a separate part of the company network and require additional building swipe access to enter a physically restricted zone. Someone in the sales and marketing team would not have access to the finance systems, they may not even be able to see the login page, if it is setup for network access restrictions. But the customer service rep may have access to the sales systems and also a window into the finance data to manage customer billing inquiries. All of this follows the principle of least privilege. Employees are only allowed, the least number of permissions that they need to function within their job role. It is like a business cultural extension into the world of IT. Anyone who has experienced the company politics of authorizations in a big organisation will also know that IT often features in the facilitation of who gets what and why. Some employees within a business move between different departments accumulating access permissions over time, and for some reason they are not asked to relinquish them, when they move on to the next team. These staff members are considered "Permissions Tourists" by some administrators and the main cause of excess permissions. They will have to face the auditor at some point.

Zero trust has introduced a hardening step to the enforcement point for access. But it has not really done anything to change the business mores of assigning permissions to staff. One definition of politics is who gets what and when. Business politics are no different. The principle of least privilege should map the way people function in business, but in the computer world. Maybe a completely secure 'computer centric' least privilege model might exist. But I think a lot of security professionals are not confronting themselves with the reality enough.

Where least privilege is associated with breaches and security incidents, does not usually figure in workers having the right permissions to do their job. Take for example, the Edward Snowden breach, where colleagues had given Snowden their access, without it being centrally issued to him. The colleagues who gave him access would explain that he needed access to do his job, so that was not a breach of the least privilege principle. And there were ways of transmitting the access without central oversight.

Maybe he did not have enough vetting. In insurance, or the civil service, they would probably have alerted the situation as a concentration risk. Where too much responsibility is given to one person and the range of tasks could have been distributed across a number of workers who could not conspire with each other to pull-off something major in the way which Snowden did. My experience of working with government agencies is a positive one and I was shocked to hear of what had happened.

When an engineer has human interactive access to production systems, it is really important that as well as least privilege, they are also not allowed to just do whatever they want in the production environment. Human interaction with systems could be argued, is the most likely reason they will fail suddenly. But also, there is a temptation if you have a key to the cupboard, to go and have a look around. After all, in some ways you are responsible for what goes on there. That is where a lot of the criminal thoughts start, in my opinion. Once the system administrator knows that they are the only person that has admin to the system and has built it according to the plan they have designed. Then it seems natural that they are the "owners", in some way. The data then could be theirs. Maybe they could explore it when they feel like it. There are many cases of rogue administrators having casual access. And after being threatened with being fired, they take sole possession of "their" systems and holding the organisation to ransom.

But remote interactive human access to the "operating system" of online production servers is becoming less frequent in North America and mainland Europe. A lot of cloud workloads are being administered using software pipelines and Infrastructure as Code (IaC). That allows devops engineers to deploy new systems and applications into the cloud environment, without a human having to gain remote access. A number of high-profile attacks against

Remote Desktop Protocol, Secure Shell (SSH) and VDI remote applications, has ensured that the appetite for remoting into systems from the internet is a highly dangerous activity. This has led recently to the application of the immutable infrastructures.

Authorized action
Examples: a user action that has been allowed, changes to data or systems, a non-human service account process has been run

Once you have a Trusted Person with a Confirmed Identity. You can assign them a role, that comes with a set of permissions. Then, if that all goes well, you can decide whether an action was authorized or not. In operating systems, like Windows or Linux, this is usually as a result of an Access Control Lists (ACL) component of the OS. With applications, it could be as basic as an "if()" conditional statement in the code. That says, "If this user is authorized, then do this". There is not much to say about the concept but it is central to the whole world of IT security. It is at the heart of all security decisions that ask, "Are you allowed?"

Separation of duties
Examples: financial payment "six-eyes" approvals, cinema tickets, software release management, change control record + JIT access, MFA

Somewhere in my distant memory, I have a vague recollection of having to work with teams of officials who were not able to speak with one another. If you work in commerce, this might sound very unusual. As there is nothing stopping you from passing small talk with anyone you come across in daily life. But if you are familiar with working in government and military. You will know that there is a strong requirement for separation of duties. That means that if you come across someone who is in a separation of duties arrangement with you. You are not allowed to speak with them freely. Nor are you able to socialise with them outside of work. It could mean that you will be arrested, or court marshalled in some cases. But why would someone go to such great lengths, to prevent the free movement of individuals within society. Well, the reason is so that some decisions and actions cannot be fulfilled without more than one party agreeing to it. Take for instance, a firewall administrator whose family is kidnapped. The firewall admin has access to allow criminals, or terrorists into the government network. If there are no separation of duties in that situation, the terrorists can put pressure on the single point of entry and get access. But if there is a second person required to open the gates, then the terrorists (or criminals) will need to locate and kidnap more than one family and hope that both admins are willing to cave in under pressure. The same goes for soldiers whose duty is to launch nuclear weapons. You may have seen in the films where they are given two sets of keys, required to launch the missiles, plus the launch code from the President.

In finance teams and banking, there are usually two people and sometimes three, required to transfer large payments, such as treasury payments, between bank accounts. Each member of the six-eyes pact has to use their token, or card reader, to contribute to a software workflow. That goes from one approver to the next, until there are enough virtual signatories to endorse the transfer.

Business Email Compromise (BEC) attacks have been used for a number of years to target senior finance figures and it is not too difficult in some cases to identify the set of required signatories from a quick LinkedIn search. If the hacker can target all the necessary staff members on the same email domain and they are all using the same computer equipment, that has the same critical vulnerability. Then using separation of duties in this situation, does not really make a lot of sense. Although they may be in different offices and might not even know each other very well. In order to prevent conspiracy to defraud their company. If they are aligned on a technical and logical front, there is not much stopping the hacker from achieving their objectives.

Developers have had a step up in business responsibilities over the past ten years. There was a time when developers just wrote software and were not allowed anywhere near production systems. Let alone being given admin credentials and using them from their development laptop. But now with the rise of the devops engineer, everything is on the table for the devops person. They have full access to everything. Usually though, the software is deployed through a pipeline and as I will mention in Chapter 8. A lot of contemporary systems use an immutable "deploy, blat and redeploy" approach. Which means that interactive access is not a blight on security. One feature of the agile devops CI/CD narrative is the use of Release Management role. When a developer wants to commit after forking their workload from the master branch (yes, I still do not really understand), they first have to get the go-ahead from the Release Manager. Who could realistically be one of the team that is nominated, as safe adult for that week. This is another form of separation of duties, that I think is great and would heartily encourage everyone to try it. If not just for the sake of learning to respect one another in the office.

Multi-Factor Authentication (MFA), sometimes called Second Factor Authentication (2FA). Is a form of separation of duties that requires the same person to response but using two different networks and devices. You may be familiar with receiving a One-Time Pad (OTP) number as a text message from your online banking provider, to verify an online shopping transaction. This is an example of MFA. For those who use VPN for work, there are mobile authenticator apps and hardware tokens, that display a string of numbers that changes over time. Some are like keys that you plug into the USB of your device and enter a pin. The device holds the keys to log you in and some are backed with a biometric fingerprint reader, for convenience.

Session fixation
Examples: visitors badge, browser cookie, CCTV, OAuth access/refresh tokens

As we covered in the section on Trusted Person and Confirmed Identity. There is another associated concept of Session Fixation. Which means that once a person can be trusted, their identity is confirmed, by some means of authentication. Then that authentication does not need to be constantly repeated. Instead, there can be some mechanism to assign and persists the right to access. This also extends into the Constancy Principle.

In the physical realm, this might mean that a staff member is vetted and then presents their passport to the security office and then they are issued an identity badge which contains their ID within a swipe card with their picture on it. This allows their authentication and associated authorisations to be carried around and persisted in the badge. The badge is the session fixation mechanism whilst they are employed.

With web technologies, the authentication might be a password that is entered and then the user is issued a cookie, or session token that is stored by the browser, in the device storage. This persistence allows the user to continue to use the website, or social media app, without having to constantly authenticate each time they carry out an action.

Issues to do with session fixation have always been a security problem. They are numerous and the subject of regular implementation testing. Sometimes it is possible to exploit some functionality on a website, to get the user to send their session token to you. This can sometimes be the result of cross-site access, used by websites to host its content across multiple platforms. The cross-site functionality is there to prevent the user from having to log into multiple platforms, simply to retrieve some additional content.

There are also other cases where session tokens can be ejected from the user for one reason, or another. This is a highly technical area and causes many developer headaches. It has been improved by the introduction of federated access providers and also JSON Web Tokens (JWT). But JWTs are currently proving to be a double-edged sword. Although the use of JWTs improves security there are number of implementation flaws in their use, that could lead to unexpected compromises. Security testing is the best way of using them confidently.

Most of the work, of most security consultants, is invested in conversations about identity and access control. So session fixation should be part of that pre-occupation and understanding how it is implemented equally so. From experience, there is a lack of knowledge in the area of session fixation, when compared to commercial access management administration.

7 THE MAGNIFICENT PRINCIPLES
input validation, logic issues, window of opportunity, statefulness, syntactical accuracy & inflexibility

Input validation
Examples: filling out a form, using regular expressions to check web parameters, a job interview

It may seem one of the simplest things, to make sure when computers communicate with each other. The values they send and receive, are in the form they are expecting. One of the most basic examples of this, is when a website has a form with text input fields. The user enters their name and address in the text boxes and presses the submit button. The webpage parameters are sent to the web server, across the Wi-Fi network. The format you may have seen in a browser URL, is called an HTTP GET request and looks something like a URL:

https://www.bbc.co.uk/account/mystuff?name=rob+hockey&address=123+london+road..

But what if instead of the address being:

"123+London+Road"

Instead the value could be:

"\/$a:\\.^eval(sh ls"

It could equally be some other random characters. If the server does not check the input value against a format checker and reject the bad input. It may just go ahead and use the value in a database lookup, or some other form of server-side computation. All sorts of things can go wrong. Let's get out our magnifying glass and take a closer look.

The server programming language may execute values that are provided as data. Sometimes, there is no separation of data and program scripting in web applications. This is a recurring theme and the cause of many web application vulnerabilities. If the server can be tricked into injecting some "escape characters" into data, like a semi-colon, a plus sign, or a backslash. The program will continue to execute whatever data is left as a script. Putting the hacker's additional functionality on the end of the application code. It seems madness that we have got to this point. When, for quite a few decades, client-server architectures had solved this issue with compiled languages such as C++ and ADA. Some of you may disagree because web technologies have made programming a lot easier and websites much more respondent and functional.

But this is where we are and there is a lot of action in this space, with recent attacks using SQL injection. That were thought to have been solved many years ago, with the improvements and antagonisms made following researcher David Litchfield's excellent work on the database intrusion. (last thing I heard; he was swimming with the sharks). But recently, SQL database injection attacks have also been found to work with bang up to date "NoSQL" databases as well. So, it looks like SQL injection is not going away any time soon. The main way of preventing it is through parameterising data queries in a safe way. Which is a form of input validation.

Other forms of input validation also play a part in preventing web application attacks, such as Insecure Direct Object References (IDOR), Command Injection, Cross-Site Scripting (XSS), Server-Site Request Forgery (SSRF); Prototype Pollution and Server-Site Template Injection (SSTI). All of these web attacks can lead to unauthorised access and can be prevented with input validation. Even still there are a lot of web attacks that cannot be prevented by input validation, such as state-machine issues, insecure deserialization and cache poisoning. Which have become more common recently.

Most input validation in web technologies is handled through calls to standard handlers that use well tried and tested filters. Some are provided as programming libraries, that are built into the programming language. Filters often use Perl Compatible Regular Expressions (PCRE), which is a descriptive language that uses text to define how a sequence of data should conform to a pattern.

The filters need to be applied and setup in the code, to represent the types of data that the program is expecting to see. So, for instance, if the program is expecting to see a date, in the UK format, it would see two numeric digits for the day of the month, followed by two numeric digits for the month and four numeric digits for the year. This could be represented in a PCRE definition as:

`^[0-3][0-9]/[0-1][0-9]/[0-9]\{4\}$`

The same approach can be used to describe and filter on a range of input data. But it is very easy to get it wrong. Most of the major programming frameworks out there, have features that help to make the process of validating input values easier.

With the age of AI language models, it should become

easier to filter out unexpected text values, as that is what LLMs do very well, by predicting what text should naturally come next and let you know if it doesn't.

Laziness or sheer exhaustion when it comes to input validation probably contributes to most vulnerabilities in early release code. Fortunately, code scanning will pick up most of the issues, if the code is scanned for security bugs. There is a developer adage that goes "all input is evil" that could also be the title of this section.

Logic issues, comprehension and confirmation biases

Examples: the guard checked that the door is still locked and therefore everything is okay, but the door could have been opened and shut again in the meantime, a server is compromised – therefore all servers are compromised

This is probably one of the most difficult concept areas to describe. I think keeping it simple and giving some direct examples might be the best way of understanding this security area that affects all aspects of life.

When I have written computer programs, and they sometimes include subroutines that iterate and transfer values between variables. There is a possibility for complicated logical failures. One example that used to be common with the C programming language is called the off-by-one error. I will try to explain. In computer languages, sometimes counting starts from zero instead of one. If I was going to loop around a iterated calculation using a for() loop in C, I could use the following code:

```
for(int x=0;x<=5;x++) { printf("%d \n ", x); }
```

This code sets the numeric variable x to equal zero. It then loops for until x is less than, or equal to five. The last value x++ increments the x value by one each time round the loop. The printf() function just prints the integer number to the console with a \n newline character. The output might look something like this:

0
1
2
3
4
5

Which seems okay, but if we were only looking to get five elements in our list, if you start counting from zero, then you have six items in the above list. And it you were only looking for five, this creates the off-by-one error https://en.wikipedia.org/wiki/Off-by-one_error.

That used to cause all sort of ridiculous bugs in software, that could take you a while to sort out. It may not sound much. But counting to six instead of five in a lot of computer systems, can be the difference between a nuclear meltdown, or a plane falling out of the sky.

Another common feature of logic in systems, results in the ability of criminals to use a system for money laundering. When criminals steal money, it is often trivial for law enforcement to track down the criminals by using the old "follow the money" technique. Cash notes have serial numbers. If someone steals millions of dollars from a bank vault, the money's serial number may all be registered. So it is not possible for the criminals to spend the money freely because the serial number range will be detected and their visits to the shops will get them caught.

But losing track of the source of the money is possible using a process called Placement, Layering and Integration. The placement phase might be something like a criminal giving money to a money mule network or spending the money in a casino. The money is put through layering in the money mule network. Where it is transferred around lots of different accounts, so it is impossible to trace back the route of the cash. It might also cross international boundaries, between countries who are at war with each other. The integration stage is where the money now appears to be legal and the criminals receive it back into a legitimate bank account, or tangible assets. That is a crude explanation of money laundering, it is probably more complicated than that.

With the use of IT systems as a means for shifting stolen good, or laundering money. Given the right ability to put cash in and take it out again, it is possible to achieve using IT. Therefore, IT security is ever more important to keep society within the legal thresholds and prevent societal collapse. Like was seen in the pre-war depression of the late 1920s. Or with the financial solvency problems that led to the 2007 sub-prime mortgages collapse.

Checking bank statements has for a long time been a way of spotting indiscretions and flaws in transactions. It is one way to spot logic issues and similar audit reports can be produced for computer systems, that show non-financial transactions and allow a specialist to detect logic flaws that might be used by criminals, to induce unauthorised behaviours in those computer systems. Some of the issues are just mistakes, or lack of perception, due to system complexity. But the effects are equally felt. System availability (valour?) and integrity are a key part of IT security.

Window of opportunity
Examples: safe that can only be opened during working hours, transactional data that is only processed by a website but is not stored, a critical software vulnerability that will soon be patched

You may have seen the movie, where the bank robber holds up the bank. The bank manager is led into the vault area of the bank, where the robber orders the bank manager to open the safe vaults. But the manager tells the robber that the door will only open in the morning. Then the dilemma sets in and creates the dramatic device for the rest of the action movie.

The window of opportunity thing rarely happens. It is a useful control but the pressure on businesses to perform in an "always on" world. Mean that taking a critical resource offline for a few hours or days is usually not on the books. Take for instance road closures, when an important person visits. That sometimes happens but far less than it used to. Some companies have been promoting nightly system downtime, to save energy for environmental reasons. This is both admirable and has security value, as hackers will have to do all their work in chunks between restarts, which they may not be able to persist at. It is more likely that nightly switch-off will cause system failures. Call me cynical but I would be interested to hear if any large organisation has had success in powering down their thousands of servers every night. Then bring them back up every morning, without any issues. Sounds like a green investment opportunity.

From a hacker's point of view, the window of opportunity is a very real concept and I would imagine something that is at the top of their thinking quite a lot of the time. If they have invested money, or time in developing zero-day exploits, that may at some point be patched. They will be thinking about doing their attacks and fitting them in. As quickly as they can, to get the best out of their expensive exploits.

Reducing the window of opportunity is the preoccupation of every support team that is tasked with applying security patches, when they are released. There is usually an uncomfortable silence around the office when the patch is first released and it take some time to work out what has to be done. To raise the emergency change request and consider whether it might potentially cause something to fall over. When the patch is applied, it is a feeling of relief, knowing that the window of opportunity is now closed, and the software is safe again.

A question that I have been asked quite a few times over the years about transactional systems, is whether there is a potential for data loss, if the system never stores any data on disk. Of course, if you know anything about how IT systems work, there is usually some way in which the attacker can get their hands on the data. One example is the formjacking attack. They could also extract the data from computer memory. There is a small window of opportunity to sneak the data out, as it is being processed.

The use of encrypted memory has moved from just being a public sector preserve, to finding its way into more commercial systems. While collecting forensic evidence as part of a security investigation, I used the Memoryze memory extraction tool, a few times, to copy the RAM from an online system. That requires SYSTEM privileges if I remember and could potentially require internal electronic signatures, if it needs kernel functions. And theoretically this sort of action could be open to attackers. In retail, the use of memory skimming malware was a very common attack, against EPOS tills. That usually run on top of some form of reduced Windows kiosk version operating system, such as Windows CE. This allows the card thief to steal card numbers, while they are being processed by the EPOS till before they are sent to the acquiring bank. The types of PCI scope data often are: PAN (debit card long number), cvv2 (three digits on the back), cardholder name and expiry date.

In a step further, the card data is obscured using encryption end-to-end. The way in which some retail companies have matched this threat is by implementing Point-to-Point Encryption (P2PE), between the Pin Entry Device (PED) that you enter your card pin number into and the acquiring bank termination point. Card stealing gangs have responded in kind by launching physical attacks where they tamper with the P2PE enabled PED and change the device firmware. If you go into a supermarket or shop in the UK, you may see that PED card payment devices are fitted with all sorts of tamperproof labels, tags and dongles. The window of opportunity is closed by only storing payment card details momentarily. But then the physical tampering becomes an issue. And staff are threatened with violence if they refuse to get involved. The window we really want to close is the one between the moment the criminal smiles, to the moment they find themselves in prison. The work of the Payment Card Industry (PCI) standards organisation is impressive in the face of much adversity. I attended their annual conference in London a couple of years in a row.

One of the developments that looked like it had promise but has not transpired yet is the cvv3 standard for cards. The cvv2 additional three-digit number on the back of the payment card is a static three digits. But with cvv3, there is passive electronic circuitry built into the card that changes the three-digit number through a sequence every few minutes. So that the window of opportunity for stealing a complete card record is seconds or minutes and would not really be a viable opportunity for carders anymore.

In the meantime, payment services such as WePay, Google Wallet and Apple Pay have been appearing. Instead of transacting persistent reusable payment credentials. Mobile networks like Apple Pay use one-time transaction tokens, that relate to your primary payment method in the background, but the transaction cannot be replayed, or reused, once the transaction has gone through. Additionally, the token only refers to the value and recipient of the transaction and there is a secondary back-channels connection between your phone and Apple network that makes the payment. In theory there is nothing there to steal, not even momentarily.

Statefulness of programs
Examples: transaction processing, ACID qualities, TOCTOU

Time-of-Check-Time-of-Use (TOCTOU) bugs happen when a software routine saves a value, in a variable, such as x =1, where x is the variable and 1 is the value that is being saved. The routine then validates that the value is correct but then the value can be changed in some expected way, before the value is used in another function.

This can lead to unauthorised code execution. It is more common than you might expect. Especially when working with multi-threaded code. Let me unpack what multi-threaded means. Microprocessors allow running processes to spawn sub-processes called "threads", that usually perform repetitive simple tasks for the main process. If you right click on the taskbar in Windows and look at the Task Manager under Details, you will see a column for Threads. That tells you the number of sub-process threads that the application process has spawned to do its Windows subtasks. Most of the applications will probably do multi-threading.

Threads use a range of features called Mutual Exclusion (Mutex), either "semaphores", or software flags, to indicate which thread is clear to proceed, to read or write a figure into a variable that is used by both threads. Exploring the logical states that a multi-threaded process can be in, is extremely complicated. In some cases, there is no realistic way to comprehend all the possible states. Now that might seem ridiculous.

Some programmers that work with complex systems use a form of testing called Fuzzing. That throws structured random values, into the input variables of a program, in order to try and create a runtime exception failure (crash). If one happens, it might be the indicator that an invalid state has occurred. Some of the effects of fuzzing are never really understood. Complex systems can be so complicated, that it is not possible to know why something happened. Only that something has to curtail the program from failing in that way again, which is usually possible.

Last year at security conferences, there was a talk by Portswigger's Director of Research - James Kettle, on the potential of breaking modern state machines, using new web techniques. He revealed that what we had started to understand, as one linear process of execution within software programs. Is far more complicated and dips into subroutines from other libraries. That again relates to instructions being issued from assembler code, at a low level. If all of this occurs in an inter-related way in a concurrent and near simultaneous occurrence, the effects can be a massive number of unexpected states. Apologies James, if I got that wrong but I think that was the general gist of it.

When I first started work at seventeen, the mainframe was the only way to do business computing. I worked two short assignments in offices where there were no computers at all, everything was done using large pieces of paper and the database was drawn as a grid using a pencil. That was the way in which they did stock inventory. It was not easy but you did not have any hassles with technology I guess. At the end of each week, I got paid in cash.

Banks were the first to identify the need to commercialise the use of Online Transaction Processing (OLTP) engines such as IBM RAC-F, that were used with Automated Teller Machines (ATM) – cash machines. Transactions had to be validated against ACID qualities (Atomicity, Consistency, Isolation and Durability). To ensure that if you made a withdrawal from your bank account, the transaction would stick. It would not get stuck between states somehow, so you were deducted the amount from your account, without getting the cash in your hand. The same thing is happening now in a different generation. Although similar rigour has been applied to the current financial software, like website shopping carts. The foundation of web IT is not aligned with the task, meaning that invalid states are making current issues of note.

Syntactical accurate & inflexible
Examples: code that executes without crashing, web requests that need every parameter correct, military chit-chat and codewords

When thinking about a physical safety, my mind automatically goes to the original safe box, with the tumbler wheel on the front. You would be tempted to put that into the same section as passwords. The person who wants to enter the safe needs to know the combination after all. But having spent a number of years having to work with very ancient safes. It is fair to say, that just knowing the combination is not enough to get the thing to open. I hope you never have the experience but when you are in a hurry and there are lots of important people watching, it is painfully frustrating trying to, firstly remember the combination. Fine, I remember that having used it a hundred times. Secondly being accurate enough to stop the tumbler at the millimetre precision required to throw the levers and bolts at the right time. It is not straightforward. This is our first example of security through inflexibility.

One of the fortunate things I have been able to witness, is where an attacker has tried to attack a system and failed. Not because they did not have a wide range of software exploits and tools. Not because they did not get a foothold in the systems. But because for some reason, their code did not run well on the target system. This is just something that happens sometimes. It could be to do with specific configuration or version. You could try again later. Often is it to do with input validation, or code syntax.

With early versions of most software, it will crash occasionally. That is why early releases are usually called Alpha, or Beta releases. When unexplained crashes stop happening, then the software house will label it "stable". Many companies will stick with the stable release, or even the major release behind that (n-1) because they know the consequences in terms of fault incidents. Hacker tools tend to be fairly immature code, on the whole. It's nice to see that sometimes the trojan exited all by itself. Probably not enjoyable from the hacker perspective. It just happens sometimes; we can try again later.

With modern web applications, there is a value in ensuring that the user has to set every parameter in its right place. As well as ensuring session cookies are set and verified and things like CSRF tokens are used and bound to user sessions, there is also additional value in being inflexible with POST parameters. If the user is being asked to change their home address, the request could also include a client ID, first and last name and some other information, that is specific to the user account. Rather than just relying on the authentication mechanism, which might be faulty. In the UK, we call this "getting all your ducks lined up". And its inflexibility might be the thing that saves you a major breach.

In the world of physical security and in various militaries, since very ancient times (we suppose) there has been an encoded language, that only the military personnel are privy to. Trying to convince someone that you have been part of their military unit, involves first passing the time of day by talking pleasantries and establishing a stress baseline. The conversation moves to past historical events in the life of the unit; interspersed with codewords, innuendos and insider knowledge. That contribute to the overall impression, that you are who you say you are. But it is possible to get it wrong, it is not an exact science. I have never been in the military, but I have seen it done enough in IT security circles, to know that it can be awkward but effective. It has probably saved more lives than lost.

8 THE CONSTANCY PRINCIPLES
layered controls, continuous state of security, immutable infrastructure, controls proportionate to risk, data durability, familiarity, silence

Layered controls – defence in depth
Examples: belt and braces, door lock and bolt, porch door and internal locked door, outer firewall and inner firewall, antivirus and intrusion detection

Defence in depth was a principle in computing that was originally a military strategy, designed to wear down a superior force by causing delays, that making an enemy lose momentum. In IT security, it promotes the use of multiple security controls in series and is typified with the public sector use of two sets of firewalls – an outer and an inner set. With a Demilitarized Zone (DMZ) in the middle. During the nineties and early 2000s, and even up until recently in some cases. This was an architectural approach that meant that even if one firewall was breached, the next set could potentially block the attacker, who was boldly attempting to kick in the front door, so to speak.

Firewalls have been for a long time been considered to be allied with one or more nation state. One firewall technology may be associated with a particular country military and in some cases may give them reasonable grounds for access without telling anyone. So having a mix of different military associated appliances, meant that no single nation had open access to all the networks. This was proven to be on the right track in 2017, when the Shadow Brokers release 'open door' exploits for the Cisco ASA firewall range. It could be assumed then that there are similar access exploits and backdoors for all the other main firewalls on the market. This is an assumption that we came across often in the early days. But perimeterised networks probably do not offer militaries the same jackpot rewards that they used to.

Some other areas where defence in depth, or layered controls are still seen, is with code scanning and web application firewalls. The code scanner will trawl through the code looking for patterns of vulnerabilities, that can then be fixed before the code is deployed into production. The web application firewall (WAF), filters incoming request traffic for potentially malicious requests and abnormal behaviours like a high request rate. In this way, the two technologies do very similar things, in preventing well-known vulnerabilities from being exploited. They do not do it simultaneously though, and there is more to be said on that subject.

Take another example of a IaaS workload, like an AWS EC2 instance. This is almost the same and analogous to a traditional Windows Server in a data centre. That might be running Endpoint Protection software (antivirus) and at the same time might have other security software running that does a very similar thing. Using a Host Intrusion Detection System (HIDS) agent, or an Endpoint Detection and Response (EDR) "map reduce" client. These all do a very similar thing in finding and stopping malware processes from executing and achieving their goal. They can sometimes be used simultaneously to increase their effectiveness.

Continuous state of security – supply chain
Examples: secure IT supply chain, secure software deployment, watchmen

One of the difficulties that I have had since the early 2000s, when some open-source projects first went live. It was possible to download the code and review it for any bugs, backdoors, or malware and then compile it and install it. Of course, in the early days, before Sourceforge and GitHub, that was a fairly obscure activity. You may ask how it was even possible. I know that I did it but it is hard to remember. I would probably say, it was typing code from books and journals. Yes really, I think it actually was.

But in the last ten years particularly, the scale of open-source projects. Especially when it comes to source code like Android, Linux, browsers and any of the major applications. It is almost impossible to review the code yourself, even with feature-filled scanners. Let alone manual review, with grep searches. I remember trying to review Firefox and Android source codes about eight years ago. I managed to manually review Keepass but that is a small and more manageable source. But it was a futile undertaking with the big projects. I think Android at that time was well over a gigabyte of source code data. Which probably equates to more than a million of lines of code. Not something you can review manually.

Added to that, there are a large number of proprietary closed source binaries in any given system. Take for instance a Wintel laptop. There might be up to a dozen drivers, for graphics, pointing device, keyboard, USB, network, etc. Any one of these could be corrupted to include persistent malware. From the time that the code is manually reviewed and signed. Until it leaves its secure storage and is hash validated (we can still do that), before installing it at the OEM supplier depot. There could be malware introduced, either manually onsite, or through other compromised software tooling on the network.

Most of the time, the victims will be unaware that anything is wrong. I remember once ordering a tablet computer from a reputable market website. When it arrived, before I even got a chance to start it up. When looking online to see what features it had and whether it could run LineageOS. It turned out that the tablet I had ordered, was one of a batch of Chinese tablets, that had malware pre-installed in the warehouse in Hong Kong. Before being shipped out to customers. Unfortunately, it did not support an aftermarket bootloader, or alternative OS, so I ended up having to discard it without even using it. Which was disheartening but at least I did not go ahead and use it knowing that it was hacked.

Let's take a moment to think about what we would want to see happen in our global supply chains. It does help to dare-to-dream once in a while. When the developer writes the driver code, the release manager checks that the test team have thoroughly checked the code for any bugs, backdoors or malware. This follows some sort of standard. Then the release manager put the company mark on the code, to say that it is bone fide and signs it securely, so it cannot be misrepresented. The engineer building the laptop, can download the code and identify it as legitimate. She installs the code on the laptop in a secure environment and does not leave it lying around in the office overnight. There is a way from the start of the build to the end, to ensure that no tampering has occurred. I think this would exemplify the sort of features of a secure supply chain arrangement. There is probably more to be said on the subject.

When considering the continuous secure state of a system, like I said at the beginning of chapter 3. We should be trying to apply logic and reason to our view of security but as humans, we often think automatically out of our subconscious thoughts and dwell too often on subliminal associations.

When you find yourself in a business meeting talking about a particular set of IT processes running on some servers in a data centre somewhere. It does not seem rational that we would be aware of intangible forces at work around them. But it is possible during the user experience and lifespan of a system to bring about complex systemic difficulties that in other cultures and in other times may have been referred to in terms of a superstition, haunting, or a curse. Whether the decisions of the business or its service delivery managers might have some adverse effect on this. Perhaps by the system causing the deaths, or misery of others. This is not something that is spoken about among IT people, in my experience. But I have heard people say some very mysterious things about IT systems over thirty years on the job.

Once I worked with a very zealous Christian IT manager who would always place his hands on servers, when he was trying to fix them and swore that on more than one occasion, they just started working again because he prayed silently over them. Believe what you will about these things. But when we receive our tech items, I think most people would prefer to receive a blessing, instead of a curse. I would want to buy a computer from someone who had a bit of positive mental attitude. Not something you can work out, without visiting the shop, or speaking with the engineering team. Do you catch my drift.

Immutable infrastructure
Examples: frozen settings, headless instances, removal of interactive access

During the mid-2000s, when a Windows Server could not be supported any longer, it was possible to apply a fixing template, variously called DeepFreeze and WinLocker (pre-ransomware). These programs would take a snapshot of the system configuration and freeze the settings, whilst still allowing the server to run. It would mean that the server could not be changed. All of the drivers, applications and system settings would stay exactly the same. This was a potent obstacle for hackers at this point. Most of the mass production malware, was based on executable processes and installing windows services. So, if you were not able to write to anywhere meaningful and not able to start any new processes, or install services. There was little opportunity to hack the server. Of course, just a few years later, most of the malware was memory resident only and injecting into existing processes. DeepFreeze would not have made much difference.

The same thing is available with cloud IaaS instances, that can be configured to not allow changes. Some features of cloud allow configuration monitoring and automated roll-back to prevent malicious changes from affecting the cloud infrastructure. There are also immutable instances, that are locked into a set configuration and cannot be changed whilst running. They have to be stopped before any changes can be made.

There is also a limitation on remote interactive human access. Preferring instead to deploy code using a CI/CD pipeline. Other cloud consistency features include blue/green deployments, where one fleet of cloud servers remains in service, while another is being upgraded and then introduced into use. Then the first fleet of server instances are removed from service. Users are gracefully redirected using an application gateway from the old instances to the new. Allowing a seamless transition between software versions. You may already be aware of all of this because it has been around for a few years. But not all security teams keep up with the current technologies. Those outside of IT probably do not know it even happens.

Another similar trait in container environments, that is quite technical, is to reduce all functionality in the container dependencies. Such as removing the shell environment, removing tools such as curl and wget. Applying Linux capability permissions, Apparmor or SeLinux, where relevant; to disallow certain executable actions and to prevent running code. Other than the intended container content. This is seeing some very effective results, and it is encouraging to see this being done as a market trend, by a whole range of devops teams, at different companies, without being driven by IT security on the whole. This is one of several encouraging moves recently. Probably more to do with hardening but makes the container immutable through lack of opportunity.

Controls proportionate to risk
Examples: cost/risk analysis, controls maturity scoring

Carnegie Mellon Maturity Index (CMMI) has been for a long time the measure of an organisations advanced state of security. With maturity of zero being the lowest and five being the most advanced. Some aerospace manufacturers have attained a five. The maturity is assessed under several categories and there is usually a radar diagram provided, that shows how the company in question has scored in each security controls category. Not all categories mature at the same rate. So, the constancy, or comprehensiveness of cover, may not be consistent across all categories. One company may be stronger at physical security but not at network security. Another company may be great at logical access control but not with web applications.

But before, the organisation or company looks at their controls' maturity. They will probably want to know whether they have any controls in the first place. When a company measures their IT risk, and whether controls are there to cover the identified risks. They will usually run to a portable ISMS checklist standard, such as ISO27001 and match their security controls against a Statement of Applicability (SOA), as not all controls are going to be applicable to the system in question. Some of the controls will be marked not applicable. The ISO27001 standard does not look at maturity, it only asks whether the control is required and whether it exists.

That is enough to satisfy the risk requirement in a basic way.

It is unclear what the actual value of ISO27001 certification is but the perceived value is tangible. Having worked in information security governance for around ten years, I have noticed a big difference between companies that do have ISO and those that don't. But I do not think it is a direct result of having the certificate. It appears to me as the cherry on top of an already existing security cake. A cake that is currently being stamped on by destructive teenagers each month. We need to double down on core security controls that matter and do our Fermi estimates, as Rick Howard describes in his excellent book "Cybersecurity First Principles", that I read last year. I think it is completely aligned with making the best of the current technologies and recommend you read it.

There are many regulations and frameworks that aim to quantify and address the various industry requirements for security. In areas such as health there is the US HIPAA health insurance act, with financial payments there are various European Central Bank laws, the Payment Card Industry Digital Security Standard (PCI-DSS), with bank transfer there is the SWIFT customer security standard. There is a new Artificial Intelligence Act. Sarbanes-Oxley (SOX) and OECD, to do with tax, financial accountability and transparency. There are many other notable standards and local laws, whose purpose is to increase the potential for organisations to combat information security risk, with respect to the industry that it applies to.

Data durability & permanence
Examples: offline backups, multiple availability zones, write-once read-many, disk arrays, sharding, in-memory databases

When a company has a vast amount of information that it needs to keep safe. Either because it is instantly useful for operational requirements, or because it can be aggregated at some point and give deep insights into the big picture and affect strategic decision making. The same fundamental needs exist. That the data needs to stay the same and not be changed in any way and also be there when you go and look for it.

At the start of the century, IT manufacturers worked hard to create data storage hardware that had minimal loss potential. The integrity of the data that is stored on the disk was so valuable, no disk faults can be tolerated. Then, new technologies like RAID were invented to duplicate the data multiple times over several disks with the same rack enclosure. So that any one disk failure would not mean that data was lost. Eventually with the advent of cloud data centres, the vastness of shared disk resources meant that disks storage could be so massively replicated over different disks that the quality of disk drives was not so important anymore, with cost taking the front position. If a drive is bad, just replace it. Sometimes this has been done with robotics.

Looking back in history, the ancient civilisations had similar challenges, with keeping hold of information. Take for instance the great library of Alexandria. It held around half a million books on all sorts of subjects, philosophy, history, religion, etc. When it was burnt down by rival Iron Age neighbours, in a fit of rage, most of the written heritage of the ancient world was lost.

Fast forward to the modern age. We have online systems and 24x7 data centres. Most of the data contained in online systems is backed up to tape drives, or alternative online storage locations. This means that even if the equivalent vandalism is wrought on those systems, there is a chance that the support team might be able to restore the data and get them back to where they were before the incident happened. In practice, a skilled attacker will also go after the backups as well. Those might be physically separate and managed under a manual process. Or they could be online and managed using the same accounts for the main production system.

Anyone who has seen the excellent Mr. Robot series on streaming video, will know that backups are within the target mindset of the hacker. Companies who use backups usually measure the effectiveness of how much data will be lost due to an outage (Restore Point Objective) and how long it takes to recover the data (Restore Time Objective). The RPO/RTO is dependent on how critical the system is. Some systems like air traffic control and trading systems can have a zero RPO/RTO. But most have at least a few hours or days. Effective offline backup is becoming the new front line against the ransomware threat and there optimal scope for a reboot of the knights of old, protecting a chest full of magtapes and other precious key treasures. One system I worked with a few years ago had potential loss value of several billion dollars, so it is not fantasy and make believe. Some national systems have risk potential for widespread loss of life. This is not child's play; it is deadly serious logistics. That probably needs military planning skills.

Availability of information is important. But so it data integrity. When information is written to storage, in some cases it cannot be allowed to change. When investigation teams want to make a note of some information they have found. In an effort to preserve evidence and ensure that the vital information was not overwritten. The use of Write-Once-Read-Many (WORM) media is crucial to keeping hold of data. Nowadays admins will sometimes use USB flash drives and although there is usually a switch that turns off write mode. The files can be easily removed or altered by switching the switch back again. Previously we would use CD-R discs that only allowed write and then you could not amend the data on the disc or remove it without destroying the disk. Back in the day, there was also magnetic WORM drives that had additional re-write protection, but I have not seen any of those for a long time. There are still technical options available but dedicated off-the-shelf is better.

Familiarity

Examples: a regular pattern of behaviour, setting baselines and thresholds for events, observing network traffic every day, security guard patrolling company premises

This principle is one that we take for granted a lot but is worth unpacking. In the UK, when strangers meet in public places, they often pass the time of day by starting to talk about the weather. It will go something like "Nice weather for the time of year" and the other person will say something like "My garden has never looked so radiant". Then the first person might say "But we might be in for some rain at the end of the month". The second person will respond "Well that would be nice as well." There is a reassurance in the simplicity of a conversation about the weather that everyone has access to it and can be assured that their perception of the baseline weather is appreciated by everyone else around them. The shared social experience is universal in the UK and grows social cohesiveness. I think it is why civic respect is still a supportive factor in rural villages around the UK. The constant support of predictable characters and weather. And the mindset behind it is a comprehension of a weather baseline and familiarity with what to expect next from people. The same goes for cyber security.

I spent the better part of ten years, every day sitting in front of a set of monitors looking at rows and rows of log data, security alerts and graphs of event trends. Obviously, most days I did other things as well, like pen testing, meetings and chatting with colleagues. After a while of looking at the same daily view of event data, you start to really notice changes and become aware when an intrusion has occurred. Getting the event data view right is the first step. You want to keep your finger on the pulse of what matters. Not all event data has the same significance for security. Choosing which data to keep on your dashboard and where to do your daily checks and searches is the important thing. After that, having an eye for what is unexpected and unfamiliar, is the skill that will spot the hack. It is a bit like carp fishing, in a way. You must set the tackle up right and fish in the right place but then you must know what a bite looks like, before you strike.

Often, I would be asked to check a colleagues work and see whether what they were looking at was in fact a hacker at work. Did they have a bite? Of course, I did not have the same view that they were looking at every day. So, it was hard to be immediately clear. But with some piecing together the events, it was possible to back up the initial indicator, with further activity, that in the end shows a full-blown attack in progress. It all starts with familiarity though. If you are aware of the context of system behaviour, the naming of systems and what they are used for. Then it is possible to know when 'out of the ordinary' behaviours occur. The SANS Institute used to have a poster called "Know normal, detect evil", which sounds a bit extreme but is basically what we are talking about in this section. Baselining is an incredibly powerful security concept. Set it up and keep watching!

There are several aspects to familiarity. One of them is understanding what is normal with computing technology, what logs are normal for a system to produce when not under attack. What do the network protocols look like in their everyday form. The second aspect is the human functional overlay. This might be dependent on the type of industry your organisation is in. In a finance organisation, there might be batch processing of transactional rows of financial figures. These might have a confidentiality importance but also an integrity and availability. You might become familiar with the fact that the stock trading floor, ships figures at the end of each day, to an analytics platform. This is normal behaviour. But what if those figures also get shipped to an online file sharing platform, at the same time. This might also be normal behaviour, but you have not seen it before, so you are unfamiliar with its real-world purpose. It would be wise to make a quick phone call and challenge it. When done well, this really builds up the security team's reputation over time.

Fortunately, a lot of system activity is tied to human user accounts, although some systems have generic service accounts. It is possible to identify an action being performed by a specific person. So you can ask that person, or their line manager, about the unusual behaviour. This is regular daily work for the security operations team. It is re-assuring to know that someone has got your back. Once in a while, I have been contacted by someone in cyber operations about online actions. They were very polite and professional. Although the actions they spotted were business related and permitted, it is good to know that someone is keeping an eye on things online. It did not bother me, and we soon got to the bottom of the matter. It demonstrates value, when done professionally.

Silence
Examples: absence of significant information

An under rated concept in security is silence. An absence of any information could be a definition of confidentiality. The Kali Linux landing screen used to have an adage that read "The quieter you become, the more you hear". Trying to convince business managers that they need less information, is something I have been doing for years.

9 THE ACTION PRINCIPLES
observability, compensating controls, contain the threat, system recovery

Observability and transparency of actions
Examples: CCTV, application logs, polygraph test, observable transactions, pattern matching, threat hunting

In my mind, the cyber detection capability is how you define the security of your organisation. "The eyes are the lamp of the soul", as the saying goes. Without the ability to see what is happening within the complexity of IT systems, it is not possible to know whether you are being exploited in some way. Detection is the starting point for any security improvements. Action leads to reality, leads to conversations that make sense and better protection. It makes sense because it is real, it's associated with tangible facts and events, that are relevant to you and your organisation. We will go on to consider the Lantern principles and none of those ideas are wholly relevant without knowing, first-hand, what is going on within your own systems. The way that IT systems have created transparency of actions for a long time, is by generating logs.

Not all actions are logged, logs are vast and complex, not easily understood but frequently documented somewhere. Logs can be modified. It is possible in some cases to avoid manipulation, such as a technique I call the 'momentary syslog of death'. The system throws out a descriptive log message across the network to the log server, at exactly the time that the system fails, or is hacked. Cloud virtualisation also offers log insights that are hard to interfere with. As they exit the operating environment through a side-channel. Modification of logs at source is not something that is often spoken about in preventative security discussions, but it is clear that it exists in the attacker's toolkit and in the evidence from real crimes. Logs do get wiped and sometimes modified. Like most secure technologies, log evidence is very dependent on known good state and safe possession. Centrally storing logs that are generated and sent immediately, is a partial fix. Having a side-channel is better.

Cyberattack detection in large enterprises follows a mostly predictable process of collecting large amounts of logs, on every type of digital process. From operating systems, access control systems, applications and networking devices. Using the aggregated logs, it is then usual to correlate events together into a patchwork that reveals a picture of what has happened. The security log management system (SIEM) will usually contain some background information in the form of log parsers, that understand the fields in each kind of log and what information is useful.

The background info will also probably include a bunch of attack signatures, for behaviours like network sweeps, bulk data movement, brute force login attempts and other combinational signatures, where two or three events sum up to a more serious event, that warrants an alert. For quite a few years it was my main concern to ensure that the right logs got delivered and alerted in some government systems.

The UK government has formal ways of defining the requirements in guidance documents, in the case of protective monitoring this was contained in the Good Practice Guide No.13 (GPG-13). It is a little out-of-date now. At one point, I was able to recite it to anyone who asked. Contemporary cloud systems will often send their logs into built-in features of the cloud platform that provide analytics capabilities. There are also marketplace add-ins for security log analytics. Many companies still choose to export their logs into a separate enterprise log management SaaS, and there are also some useful managed mSOC Security Operations Centres out there.

Much of this type of detection and response is likely to be fully automated with AI in the next few years. But for the several hundred IT suppliers that I have reviewed for security over the past five years, this is not something that is mainstream right now.

From around 2003 to 2013, I guess. It was possible to define a fairly static pattern and then match it against a file, or a network data stream. The pattern would effectively match and allow you to stop malicious traffic and content. With pattern matching definitions like the ones described in the input validation section. It was a complete and foolproof way of spotting attacks. There was confidence in its effectiveness. It seems fairly ridiculous now, that we were dependent on this approach and that it was effective. Of course, pattern matching still has some effect in discovering bad. But it can no longer be depended upon on its own. The attackers have found numerous ways of circumventing the visibility of their attacks. But surprisingly, the use of them is intermittent with some attacks being very easily detected in circumstances, where there is unlikely to be any advanced detection and response capabilities. If an attacker was attempting to break into a high security system, they might employ network obfuscations, log sanitisation and rootkits. But to mess about in the systems of the local tyre centre, or florists, they might not even bother with covering their tracks. Unless they were teenagers.

Pattern matching is not a new thing, we have an innate way of seeing patterns in randomness and giving it a name. I have worked with several analysts over the years who have the ability to see patterns in random data. Some of my colleagues have been helped in this by being on the spectrum. And when going deep on incident response, I have also trained myself to be able to see patterns in data, when looking at a wall of monitors. It helps if you know what you are looking for. It isn't magic, or to quote Hugh Jackman in the film Swordfish, "I just see the code in my head". You would probably need a computer science degree, ten years of programming experience and lots of time looking at PCAP packet captures. But I can see people's jaws drop and their face colour drain when I start explaining what I am looking at. They nod and say, "yes, I see". There is the gulf between those who know and those who really could do with understanding. Many of those who know what they are looking at are not able to explain what it means, to the people who most need to know.

Sometime around the early 2010s there was a new development in CCTV surveillance that used machine learning to automatically analyse moving pictures of people walking and measured the way in which arms, legs and torso moved together. This was introduced as gait detection. Using the way in which a human's body moves, to create a statistical likelihood, that matches a known set of recorded gaits. The statistical modelling of the body movement is not a fixed signature pattern, like file patterns or iris contours. Or in the former static patterns used in Intrusion Detection Systems (IDS) and Antivirus (AV) systems. The development of dynamic patterns, that change over time, is a more advanced way of recognising things like human behaviour. Like a pen and paper signature that someone signs on a bank cheque (check). It takes into consideration, things like injuries, adaptions in baseline behaviours and people acting slightly out of character. Such as wearing a disguise or acting out of character. It also is affected by age and mental health.

One of the main difficulties with observability in networks recently, has been the more widespread use of HTTPS encryption and the greater need to ensure that browser connections are not intercepted maliciously. This has led to the ability of some organisations to struggle in providing full packet capture and network interception for the purpose of checking network traffic for malware or data leaving an organisation.

Around ten years ago, I suppose there was about 50% of traffic that used encryption but now, most meaningful browser traffic is encrypted, maybe as much as 95%. There is still an amount of browser traffic that is unencrypted for performance reasons. But web developers have come to understand that even though data might not be sensitive in the unencrypted leg of a communication, the rest of the encrypted traffic might be undermined in some way by exposing another part of the total session.

Nowadays, the advice it to just encrypt everything using HTTPS and use HSTS to ensure that it stays that way. But it means that in some cases, it is not possible to get incidental observation of what is going on within a private network. You need to deliberately add an observation break in the encrypted channel, and this introduces a confidentiality weakness.

Compensating controls
Examples: Reactive automation playbook in serverless cloud, fire suppression system, purely reactive mitigations, lockdown

When a middle-aged man buys a sportscar, people may say he is compensating (I drive a Jaguar). For not reaching the full extent of his male maturity, no less. But that is not what we are talking about here. "Compensating controls", is a category that made it in to the ISC2 CISSP security professionals' qualification and is defined as "*Compensating controls reinforce or replace normal controls that are unavailable for any reason. These are typically backup controls and usually involved higher levels of supervision and/or contingency plans*". So they fit into a layered approach to risk, as an action of last resort.

In the UK, the general public are not allowed to carry guns. You would automatically receive five years in prison, for having a handgun without a license. But I would suggest that if guns were allowed again. Strangely, I remember playing with guns as a child. Well then, a sidearm would probably fit into the category of a compensating control. If all the planning and logistics have not worked, the president is lying on the floor dead, then waving guns around could work for the photo shoot. But it may not change the situation. Guns should definitely be considered a compensatory control and also an action of last resort and not foremost in the security planning schedule. In my dumb opinion. But then sometimes you need an action of last resort - a fire suppression system, a lockdown, flashing red light and a gun. And a Hollywood film director, to film you slowly walking towards the camera with wet hair.

Getting back to cyber, when a data centre manager is planning out his installation. There is no room for fire hazard. Most data centres have huge halls, full of racks, with electrical and electronic equipment. Any one of those pieces of equipment can consume the same amount of electrical charge, as a spin dryer, or a hot water tank. If one of them loses ground and a capacitor bursts, it could spray sparks all over the place. If the server room is full of cardboard boxes and debris, soft tissue and grease lubricants, it could quite easily lead to a fire.

Consequently, most data centres have a strong Foreign Object Debris (FOD) policy. But if all else should fail. There is usually a pre-charged fire suppressant system. Where the water is already in the pipes already waiting to burst out, as soon as it senses a fire. Some more extreme cases, there is a Halon (or equivalent) system that extracts all the oxygen from the room and locks down the exits. If you are caught inside the server hall when the Halon alarm goes off, it can be pretty scary. You have a couple of minutes to get out of

The action principles

the hall, before basically you die a horrible suffocating death. Or they switch off the suppression system and save you. I didn't do anything.

Most data centres no longer use this approach, which is a relief. Halon is also poisonous but that won't matter because you will already be dead from having no oxygen for the past hour. I heard of one person once who it happened to and I am sincerely sorry to anyone who knows someone who has passed away in this way. You have my sincere apologies.

One of the compensating controls which we have all had to go through recently (apart from Sweden and parts of Africa) was the global pandemic lockdown. This was an action of last resort, while a more lasting control - the vaccine, was developed and rolled out. Realise that this can be a divisive subject, so moving along. What I am trying to get to is about cloud security.

With the increased adoption of cloud IT, a lot of effort goes into ensuring that cloud guardrails are applied and the excellent work by the CIS Security company, has done a lot on this to develop benchmark standards. This has driven cloud service providers to also produce their own guidance on keeping cloud safe, on both sides of the shared responsibility model.

Serverless and container deployment models have further increased security through configuration hardening and the streamlined execution processes that they provide. On top of all this useful preventative security, there is cloud monitoring and reactive playbooks that use automation, to jump in and fix issues, as they occur. This could be for example, where a container generates a log when it is asked to start a command line shell, or run a bash shell command, like "wget https://badstuff.ly", that is unexpected. A point of last resort automation can be setup to listen, for any shell commands that are unexpected and if they happen. It can execute a range of compensating actions. Such as removing the pod from the node/cluster, adding a network or service policy, setting an allowlist deny at the perimeter. These compensations act to block the attack in progress. Giving the support team enough time to work out what happened and put in a more lasting fix.

There are lots of things to be said about cloud automation as a compensating control and there will be some very varied and passionate opinions on the subject. I recognise, I have probably not said enough and those who know about it will continue to use their passion to develop this important field of work.

Contain the threat
Examples: separation from the threat source, logical path to recovery is unhindered, no sign of threat progressing, regaining control over systems, threat source is removed

We are talking about ideas and theoretical concepts; dare I even say philosophies of design. This sounds sketchy and not the practicality we expect from IT. Which after all is a very practical science-based industry. But when it comes to principles like "Contain the Threat", I have heard some really sweeping statements, that do not resonate with the reality of eradicating advanced threat actors, from vast organisations, with thousands of complex systems. Sometimes it might seem more reasonable to say something like "All we have to do is heal human nature and remove all the greed and hate".

What most IT leaders mean, when we start talking about having an incident, is to be able to make the problem go away. That is not the same technically as containing the threat, in my opinion. I was fortunate enough to get out of the frontline of security operations after ten years in 2013. With brief occasional revisits, over the next five years. Which coincided with the emergence of the ransomware threat. For me, the ransomware threat has not gone away. Simply by working in another area of security governance instead. But generally, I do not think about ransomware threats all that often. This may sound crazy to a SecOps team. But the ransomware playbooks are already defined to meet the ransomware threat and are maintained by the operations teams in real-time, every day. With new IoT signatures appearing all the time. There is a great deal of governance involved but fortunately that is not my daily concern. Just in case you were thinking of joining the security industry but did not fancy having to do hostage negotiation all the time. Not everyone is obsessing over ransomware, there are other threats and duties to perform. That probably does not sound good to a CEO, who loses sleep over ransomware all the time, but it is reality. There is more to IT security than just ransomware. It is just the most visible and impactful threat for businesses right now.

In the physical world, we might go to a pub (or bar) and see a couple of men fighting and decide to step in and restrain our friend from doing something stupid. This is a bit like containing the threat. The issue may have been hiding for a while, but something has kicked-off and the issue has been revealed. Some damage or loss may occur. But fortunately, Shiela was able to restrain her brother. They are still standing there and both angry. They might decide to push through again and do some harm. The threat is still in the building. So it is not an eradicated or fully recovered situation. That is containing the threat.

With security incident response in traditional data centres, online services, or in self-hosted cloud. If there is trouble detected. It first has to be identified as a security incident. This is usually called the triage stage, where we are not really sure if something is kicking off. They lads might just be excited. But when an incident is declared, it could be by raising an Major Incident ticket with the organisations incident ticketing system. Then usually the incident response team, that is often cross-disciplined and on standby will kick in. A bit like volunteer firefighters, who are on-call.

When I have been involved in security incidents, usually

the first response is to isolate the affected device, or part of the network. With traditional networked data centres, this can be straightforward. You go to the data centre and pull out the cable. With self-hosted cloud, it is a little more difficult, if there is also account compromise of some kind. In some cases, the compensatory controls may have kicked-in, or a runbook scenario creates the appropriate isolation automatically. Accounts can be disabled, to prevent them from continued use. In some cases, bringing down the public internet access may be necessary. You may think this is the end of the world and what would the company directors think. But having been at the forefront of more than one hundred investigations, some of which were incidents, and a few which became major incidents. The directors of a company understand unplugging the internet. They maybe don't understand some of the other things that you would like them to consider but unplugging the internet is something that gives them control. It is usually a safe proposal. I would think carefully whether you want to make the internet optional. As quite a lot of the rest of the process will depend on that decision.

Incident response process is usually fully documented in large organisations and the CSIRT/CERT Computer Emergency Response Team, will have a clearly defined path to resolution. After identification of the incident, triage and the containment stage (contain the threat), next comes the full recovery operation. But before that happens, it is important to work out whether the threat really has been contained. This is what I started this section by explaining. The concept is simple, but the technology is not, absolutely not simple. The initial indicator that there was a compromise was the hacker not trying too hard to cover their tracks. When they become aware that they are being investigated, the game changes very quickly and they can either drop the goods and run. Alternatively, they may decide to install some very oblique persistence, in an unthought of part of the network, a printer, or HVAC system controller - perhaps. Then everything goes quiet for a week, or a month. So, you have fixed the initial access point, continued to monitor but there are no more indicators coming from the initially affected devices and applications. When you choose to release your hold again is crucial. Many organisations will choose to just keep everything in lockdown until the problem is fixed up watertight. I guess it is a case of risk versus reward, for your customers and other stakeholders.

The most frustrating aspect of some impacts, that never quite make it to becoming a security incident, are where some functionality is obviously broken. I used to go on the rule of thumb that nine times out of ten, an incident would be a fault. With only one in ten occasions being a security incident. And that averaged out reasonably well. It does not mean you should not investigate every issue and try to get to the root of it, this is known in IT support, as the Root Cause Analysis (RCA) and there is a whole bunch of science behind it. But where there are annoying things that are broken and they affect a company doing business, we call that an impact of some sort. Then the loss of control can be an indicator that a threat is loose. This is frustrating because without the correct diagnostics and debug logs, being able to apply testing experiments. You will often not know whether it is sabotage.

This is becoming more urgent with the increased use of SaaS applications, where the company consumes the online application as a user and has no control of the software, or underlying infrastructure. It either works, or it does not. The company that provides the SaaS may have an obligation to investigate support issues. But the contract may not cover feature requests and fixing obviously broken features. Actually, it should always cover fixing broken features. What is support for anyhow. To complete the analogy, you leave the pub (or bar) and go back to your car, only to find a large scratch up the side of it.

I mentioned at the start of the book that it sometimes feels like cyber defenders are fighting a losing battle, against an adversary who has increased in skill, greater than organisations have been able to protect themselves. The area of containment is one such area. It is going back ten years, to the point when I started to get the losing feeling. As an example, when fighting off an active attack within an organisation, it is sometimes necessary, even now, to shut down a device quickly. With a laptop, you used to be able to manually reboot Windows in a way that would completely reset all processes. To the state that they started from on the hard drive. But at some point, it was decided that the default reboot action with Windows should be a hybrid restart. Which means that some malware can survive the reboot. You can change this with a registry entry, but it did not help if you find one in the default state.

Couple this with the laptop manufacturers move to including multiple batteries in a laptop. For a while I used to remove the battery from my laptop and use a lose cable, so if I recognised that I had clicked on a malicious link, during an incident investigation, I could instantly pull the cable and not download the malware. It sounds paranoid but it actually worked to prevent annoying rebuilds, on more than one occasion. It was possible to check the gateway, network and NIDS logs to confirm this kind of near miss. A crucial five second intervention time on a slow network, is the difference between being hacked and not being hacked. But that is no longer possible.

Also, at some point Windows servers started asking you for reasons why you wanted to reboot a server, and I would be sitting there thinking, if I can restart this service in the next ten seconds, things would be a lot better. But I can understand why things like this happen. It is for the reasons given in chapter 2 and based on prioritising user experience over security necessity. It is frustrating and there are many things like this that have happened that affect the security response. But with the increase of automation these sorts of manual interventions are not on the books anymore. Which contributes to the finality of actions, that come with physical or direct intervention. I remember going around an office full of computers inserting removable media and hitting ALT-F4+ENTER more than a hundred times to try and control a incident from bricking them. It was physically tiring but came with a satisfaction that I was hitting the nail on the head, so to speak. Most hammers now come with a built-in screwdriver. Whose idea was that?

One feature of laptops which fell by the wayside a few years ago, was the hardware switch on the side. That allowed you to physically disconnect the radio circuitry and Wi-Fi interface. Not sure why that is not still a feature. I guess it is because the number of support calls saying that the Wi-Fi was not working, and they did not know about the network on/off switch. So instead of better labelling, or making the feature more obscure, they just removed the ability to physically isolate the network. Therefore, making any incident response reliant on logical software settings, that could fall under the control of a hacker across the network. Things like this contribute to frustrating the response effort.

Also, there was a security advantage in using wired Ethernet networks instead of Wi-Fi. But obviously Wi-Fi networks are much more convenient. I use them all the time for personal things nowadays. But going back a few years, especially with providing out of hours response. In one house, I drilled through five solid interior walls, just to run an Ethernet cable through. Just so I did not have to wrestle with the suspicion that Wi-Fi might have been hacked. Another development now is that access routers no longer have flashing LEDs on the front to show that you are transmitting. It is only a small thing, and it can get a little paranoid but it all helps when trying to contain a threat.

System recovery
Examples: system reset to a restore point, achievement of a known good

state, all processes running as expected, vulnerability is patched and tested

"Everything in its right place" is a track from the Radiohead album "Kid A". With system recovery, that is exactly what we are looking for. A nice resemblance of normality. Everything is okay… mommy loves you. That sort of thing. Maybe some PTSD counselling. I have probably done as many counselling sessions as I have done investigations and would recommend that is a good ratio.

In big cities, trendy folks will sometimes call in a Feng Shui consultant, after someone has committed a serious crime in their apartment. It is not enough just to pick up the broken picture frames, rearrange the sofa and clean the carpets. Fundamentally, something has happened, that has unbalanced some unseen aspect of our consciousness, and we need to redress the balance.

Similarly, with major security incidents, it takes some time to ward off negative energy. You may have managed to "contain the threat", so you are satisfied that the hackers have not been seen in the logs recently. And they are not progress with their attack inside the organisation. All the obvious routes in and out have been shut and all processes and data are accounted for. That is nearly impossible and possibly unnecessary. But we use emotional self-regulation and psychological strokes in times of distress, so this could be excused, as necessary collective behaviour, during an emergency. But it should be clear that what we say about containment and what we mean are different and I hope everyone gets that. Everything has networking, all the accounts can be used on all the things. Where does it end. I have worked with some of the most secure systems in the world and there are always weak indicators of compromise, even in the most secure systems. Ghosts are everywhere but we must try to be rational. There has to be a path to normality, that is what we expect, and everyone is in agreement. Please try to relax.

The next task is to completely rebuild, or cleanse affected systems, as the NIST SP 800:61 Computer Security Incident Handling Standard puts it, "Recovery may involve such actions as restoring systems from clean backups, rebuilding systems from scratch, replacing compromised files with clean versions, installing patches, changing passwords, and tightening network perimeter security (e.g. firewall rulesets, boundary router access control). Higher levels of system logging, or network monitoring are often part of the recovery process. Once a resource is successfully attacked, it is often attacked again".

There is no point in completing all the redecoration and refitting work without ensuring the criminals cannot return and vandalise the same things the following week. The audacity of some hacking groups is notorious. They will use ancient psychological warfare moves, quoting the Chinese Sun Szu "Art of War" and the like, in order to unsettle you. Actually as a side note, on two occasions the hackers I investigated, referenced children's characters in their attack. Which makes me think they were immature (obviously) but also trying in some way to reassure themselves, rather than psychologically disturb their adversary (me). It made me feel almost protective of them. Stupid kids getting into something serious. In incident response, factoring in the human aspects of criminality is a must.

I am not a trained criminologist, but I can understand, if an administrator leaves an organisation in a foul rage. They have the means, motivation and time to severely punish their former employers. Then it would be more effective to go after that person, rather than waste time fixing and re-fixing the technical damage. If the rogue administrator who left, made sure they could always be one step ahead of the recovery team. The recovery is likely to be rough at best.

One underestimated action of the recovery phase is removing malware. This may sound straightforward but often it will embed itself in systems in a way that makes it very hard to remove. On a few occasions, we have had to make the call to just use new hardware. As it was not possible to completely extract the attackers code from the device. It could be that the code was running in video, or network drivers; in UEFI subsystem, or a lights-out controller (tech). Some of these areas are not within support teams' gift to troubleshoot or restore with a chip harness. In that case, it is certainly reassuring just to buy new hardware. But that comes at a cost. I think the most recent estimates for the total cost of a major security incident at a large company, are in the region of $4.2m. Which has to take in hardware costs, as well as legal bills. Fortunately, with cloud infrastructure, all of that is already done for you by the cloud vendor.

When the initial access point for an attack is identified, that could be a range of things, such as a user login that was misused. It could be access to an insecure Wi-Fi access point, or some device that fell into the wrong hands. Very often it is an internet facing web application. But most commonly it will be a phishing email. I think the figure is around 38% of attacks, according to Kevin Mandia at the RSA conference last year. Phishing in some regions is the first step to getting into an enterprise's systems. With application, desktop or mobile vulnerabilities, the recovery could be straightforward. To remove the malware, apply the necessary patch, change the credentials and then deal with all the legal and business fallout. While monitoring the situation. Sounds easy enough.

10 THE LANTERN PRINCIPLES
soothsaying, public communications, security training, security guidance, system documentation, testing and vulnerability disclosure

Soothsaying
Examples: Internal social media engagement, water cooler chats, attending meetings, tabletop planning exercises

You may have noticed in these principles there is no mention of governance. This is because the assumption is that behind all of these principled concepts, there is some decision making and intelligence steering the whole thing. We communicate, educate, train, discover, document and eventually decide. By the way, this is not a security control set and should not be used as one. Instead, we are exploring the world of security ideas and governance is always there. I have never met a security professional who did not think that there should be someone in charge. And did not want to become more involved in decision making within the organisation.

There was a move about seven or eight years ago where most security professionals migrated from a mindset of being dictatorial and enforcing their company to implement better standards. Like security staff are some kind of internal police force. We went from that position, to using control frameworks to help business leaders identify and manager their risks. This is a subtle shift in responsibility, between the security team owning the security risk and the business leaders, who are in fact legally accountable. To start allowing them to understand and accept their cyber risk decision. As the owners of the business. Even though often they need help understanding the issues.

The security employees, right up to the CISO role are all staff members. In the UK, staff have legal protection, in the form of vicarious liability, that dates back a long way. This means that an employee could be fired for being grossly negligent. But rarely will they be made financially liable for the company losses. I would not trust that is the case anymore and there are many more cases now where CISOs and other senior managers are undergoing private law suits. Concerning negligence and covering up the true state of their company's cyber security failings. It is not clear where this is going. I was looking at CISO job adverts last year. But I have decided to stop doing that, until the legal position is clearer.

For this section, I went for 'soothsaying' as an archaic term, defined since ancient times as divining, or prophesy, with an emphasis on magical, or supernatural abilities. In colloquial terms, it is often used to mean someone who pacifies the crowds with an elaborate story. I think you get where I am going with this. A major aspect of cyber security has become dispelling the complexities of the technical science, by adding a layer of marketing and also fine-tuning perceptions, through managing the narrative. Having a chat and making it better. That sort of thing. Perhaps this approach could have caused us the issues we are currently having with CISOs?

For the past seven years, most of my daily working efforts have been speaking with IT teams and their numerous IT suppliers about their new system projects and what security looks like for them. Helping them to understand and manage their risks, before anything bad happens. It is really satisfying to point out something that obviously appears wrong to a security professional and because you have built up a "we're on your side" type of rapport. They will take your word for it and go and fix the issue. Not because you are going to make their life difficult. But because you have learned to understand each other. Maybe you can even help them out by telling them what they need to do fix the issue. In some cases, security teams are now getting hands-on and doing the engineering work for system owners. Some of my own security colleagues are starting to do that as a cross-disciplined squad, or guild. A few years back I did quite a bit of cloud training and passed the AWS Solutions Architect Associate exam. I would recommend that all security executives do that, to stay connected to reality.

Social media is not my favourite subject. I do not have any active social media account, if you were trying to hunt me down online. Looking up interesting strangers used to be acceptable behaviour. But now it can be considered stalking. But anyhow, it was getting too much of an overhead with all the other things I was trying to manage. Quite a lot of people I have met have said the same thing. I still keep a LinkedIn account but that is more of a necessity than a nice to have.

My adult children disagree completely. Their whole life has been built on Club Penguin, Snapchat, Instagram and TikTok. But for me also internal social media engagement, whatever the latest version of that looks like. It can be a helpful way of security teams engaging and staying engaged with other staff in the organisation. This is not the same as public communications, or formal training. It's just colleagues getting to know how each other operates and what our motivations are. This is a subtly different to comms or training and I am calling it soothsaying, or maybe thought leadership, you could call it schmoozing, or getting alongside people. It is probably the most effective way of changing the culture of security within an organisation. Some people might say this is just talking with people. That is also true. It is always better to talk with people in person one-to-one, I think anyway.

Public communications

Examples: security news interviews, company newsroom releases, regulator statements, government legal policies

When IT security response first started out big time, probably during the late 1990s. There were very few incidents that got high profile visibility. When I started at Citibank as an network technician in 1996, the US side of the business had recently experienced an attack. That before it happened was unheard of. A hacker had broken into the bank from the internet and stolen $10m and it was a matter of very grave concern. Was this now the new normal and there was an air of disbelief. At the time, I had not yet got into the world of IT security, but I remember that it had an effect on how I perceived the systems I was working with. Up until that point, there were no real serious known cyber threats against big corporations. Sure, someone will write in about that. There were a couple of viruses, worms and annoying pop-ups on home computers but nothing in the business psyche had appeared up until that point. The news story made the papers. There were obviously no websites. Not that anyone in business was looking at. Everyone got their news from paper newspapers, from the newsagents, first thing in the morning. There was some TV news and radio of course. At some point during the day, they might pick up their newspaper and have a look at it. The Citibank robbery was in there and you could go to a library and search for it on microfiche, if you missed that daily news. Microfiche was my internet search for a few years.

At some point soon, there is likely to be a divergence of public use of online services. There will be those who use AI to replace a large part of their thinking and working stuff out, with what the AI decides is the reality. They will just accept everything it says as accurate, once GenAI gets past its

The lantern principles

teething stages and hopefully we can avoid world war in 2024. There will also be those who do not accept what anyone is telling them, on face value but will instead look for intrinsically true indicators and use rules of thumb to work out what is happening in the world around them. There have been similar people going against the public messaging all throughout history. They are usually a bit deranged but that is what a little bit of truth can do to you. But now we are in the thick of the information age, that is even more important. Hug a tree.

When a company has a security breach, the management team will decide what is in the best interest of their customers, their company and shareholders. They might also factor in what is best for the public at large and what puts them in a better strategic market positioning. This is all standard stuff, that was in place a long time before IT security came along. But what has changed in the last ten years is the willingness to see public communications as a positive force, not to be feared, if it is used in a proactive and open way.

So instead, big corporations will put their attractive representative onto the television news, to tell their customers about issues. Instead of releasing carefully worded canned soup, about increased responsibility and reviewing the evidence. They will instead give the facts, even if the issue is not fixed. It appears that sharing the reality works from a PR point of view. Over the last twenty years I have been to the Infosec conference in London about eight times. I would recommend it to anyone who wants to be encouraged, that someone is doing something about cyber security. There is a lot of noise and bustle. Hundreds of vendors, talks and workshops, on all sorts of subjects. Generally, it is free for business people with advanced booking. Some of the talks on public communications have really changed over the years. The war stories about public communications attempts have change in approach dramatically.

My personal recommendation would be to let customers

know, if there is an incident, if the incident will affect their lives, greater than their feelings of being out of control and panicking about what to do about it.

Do they need to fix anything themselves? Are they obliged to know from an ethical, practical, or legal perspective? There is real emotional trauma in finding out some institution that you trusted has turned out to have betrayed you or failed in that trust. In the UK, we have been hearing recently about the way in which the UK local Post Offices had suffered injustice from central office technical issues. Hundreds were fired or imprisoned, some died because of the issue not being made transparent to all stakeholders. I think it is important to be clear from the start if there were any failings. If someone has gotten access to your email provider, the public should be told. I can think of dozens of negative outcomes that could arise from not knowing that your confidentiality had been breached in a major way like that. Email is also still one source of identity for a whole host of services, including banking and social media. But handling public comms well can be done.

Take for instance the Twilio breaches that happened in 2023. The service desk staff received SMS text messages on their phones with a fake login URL, pretending to be their company access provider. Some support staff clicked the link and were redirected to a fake login page. They entered their company admin credentials and then authorised the session using multi-factor authentication. The connection had been intercepted by the fake login and in the background, the attackers were now connected to the real login page access. The attackers could then start a web session with any online service the company login allowed them into, over the internet. Most companies use Single Sign-On (SSO) and a federated access provider because there are so many applications, it makes sense to only manage one set of credentials for the majority of them. SSO is not ideal for everything. Anyhow, we digress.

The Twilio public communications were spot-on in my opinion. They could not have done a better job of letting everyone know what had happened. How they had handled it and what the impact to customers was, were all well explained. As it happens, there was another attack soon after and some uncertainty, but I think that overall, comms were handled really well. Don't get me started on admins using mobile phones though. It just seems very wrong to me.

Security training & guidance
Examples: instructor led classroom training, university degree, awareness blogs, websites and social media feeds, online learning, threat intelligence bulletins,

Whilst reading Dan Jones' book 'Powers and Thrones' about the history of the Middle Ages. I came across a mention of a book "Maurice's Strategicon". It was the manual for Roman officers, from the Eastern conquest of the Byzantine era, for around a thousand years. Think about that, you could say it was the mainstream security training manual in the Roman world, for about a thousand years. But of course, it was just focused on military. If you wanted to protect your fleet of merchant ships from pirates, or your chain of inns from brigands, then you would probably need to use a combination of shrewdness and undisciplined aggression. Some of the main points in that strategicon, are about how to organise a battle, how men should be equipped and behave. There are tactics for fighting certain types of peoples and it gets quite technical in some places. Not completely unlike this book. You probably would not have found the fine ladies of the villa reading it.

IT security training can be really dull. I have previously organised two training sessions and many quick knowledge shares on various security topics. To begin with you get a few people who are really keen on security, and they will stick with you through the course. Then there are a few managers who are deeply concerned. Most of us can guess why they are there. But we do not want to ask too many questions. Then there are those who have been forced to attend, who have no interest in the subject at all. I try to focus my efforts on those people, because I know that if I can keep them engaged and thinking about it, they will get there in the end. After all, cyber security is number one on the World Economic Forum threats forecast this year, as a non-technical staff member told me last week. If you care about business, you should be interested in learning about IT security, at least from a business perspective.

Security training as an idea or concept is not very, er, shall we say 'philosophical'. You have some learning objectives, some facts you need to get across and then you just give them the facts - using slides, videos and animations. Maybe play a few games, using gamification techniques. If you are old fashioned like me, you could go and read a book and have a chat with someone who knows about it.

Some of the sources of threat intelligence and security news have really impressed me in the way they have developed over the past ten years. But then some of them have backed off, either for financial reasons, or to concentrate their efforts on doing some real work in fighting cybercrime. The Daily Swig was a really useful web hacking site, that unfortunately had to retire. Some have been involved in war. ThreatPost, for example, was a great news website but got swept up in the Ukraine conflict. There are also loads of online training websites on Youtube, like the annual DefCon, RSA and Blackhat videos. Newscasts like ThreatWire and Hak5. The excellent LiveOverflow videos from Fabian Faessler. He is one of the very best in the world at explaining technical security concepts.

Organisations that are really serious about identifying advanced hacking groups, will often pool their resources using threat intelligence automation feeds, that use sharing standards like STIX and TAXII. Allowing the tools to immediately start detecting new emerging threats, as the indicators are identified by other partner organisation sharing information, through the online threat service.

For at least the last ten years, I have thought about IT security all day, every working day. It comes with obsessive thoughts that make it hard to unwind. The last major holiday I had, I read a six-hundred-page book on the Middle Ages, to just think about something different for a change. The sources of useful security information have grown in the past few years. Even the major headlines are almost too much information for one person to take onboard.

Nearly every day I will briefly review a collection of around twenty security news websites, and this is supplemented by threat intelligence bulletins. That mostly contains what I have read in the news a couple of days later but with some additional background from suppliers and subscription sources. I used to subscribe and follow public social media channels and go looking in security messaging feeds. But it very quickly turned to weaponised disinformation and almost caught me out a couple of times. Not something I have time to challenge and untangle during the working day. No, the Russians are not invading, and I do have some actual work to do today.

System documentation
Examples: documentation

Most IT admins are reluctant to write documentation. It is really important from a security point of view to know your systems better than your adversary. Hackers are excellent at the reconnaissance and enumeration stages of a cyber-attack. Finding out everything that is available to know about their victims. They are able to manage this information using open-source databases and tools like Maltego - that catalogue the vast features and naming of everything. Sometimes using the online tool Shodan, to identify systems, that may not be in production anymore. That have fallen out of the patch regime but are still available over the internet. All of these types of issues can be helped through having better documentation, inventory keeping and regular audits. Because even if you have forgotten about unsupported systems, your enemies have not.

Documentation is the key to solving most of the problems of security because it is in the documentation phase that you start to get control of the details of your systems. Remembering the saying "the hand that rocks the cradle, is the hand that rules the world". Having better information about your systems than your enemies and keeping a tight ship-shape over everything, means that you have more personal authority. But it does not make your clean t-shirt bulletproof. That is worth remembering. Make sure that you document everything, in a way that is pleasant and interesting. You owe it to yourself and the rest of the world. Have a shower and do your documentation.

Testing and vulnerability disclosure

Examples: code scanning, software composition analysis, web scans (DAST/SAST), infrastructure scans, penetration testing, red teaming, bug bounties, disclosure programs

If there is anything wrong with the garden, you get out your pruning shears and nip it off. In England, we have been fastidious in keeping immaculate gardens, since the gardening boom of the 17th Century. Some of the gardens near where I live, in Dorset, England, have been maintained in good standing since the abbots of Glastonbury arrived in the 11th Century. Ensuring that gardens are presentable, and everything is neat, is absolutely nothing like software vulnerability management. But you would think that it is, if you spoke with some developers. On the contrary, if you asked the developers to adjust the software configuration of a SpaceX capsule in mid orbit around Mars. Change the firmware of a servo driver in a nuclear reactor, or add a few lines of code to a air traffic control system. That might make them sit up and think about the seriousness of what they do. There is a disconnect between software bugs that affect security and the things that happen in real life. No less in finance companies, than in government or any other industry. It has an overall effect on the lives we live.

When working in government, the threat potential that you deal with is vastly greater than in individual private sector companies. Some of the threat impacts are measured in terms of widespread loss of life, collapse of the financial institutions, national standing with other countries (wars, etc.) and the list goes on. So, if you have an open source project, such as all the trouble that was had with Log4j libraries. Then you could find yourself fixing a trivial technical bug, in the software. That actually has the potential to exterminate all life on earth. Time for sober thinking. But it never really crosses the developers mind, when they are asked to fix a few lines of code.

Software Composition Analysis has been around for a while, and it is a way of discovering what supporting libraries and imports that a piece of software uses. This is especially important with containers as they use nesting to hide containers inside containers and some of the nested containers may not have been patched somewhere down the line. SCA rips everything apart and works out whether anything has a patch missing. Really neat. It has also been built into features like Docker Scout, which can make developers lives easier.

DAST scanners are dynamic and scan the online website from outside, usually while the web application, or Single Page Application (SPA) is in a temporary staging platform. It picks up on OWASP types of vulnerabilities, using signatures and can find a range of security bugs.

Code scanners, SAST and manual code reviews, look at the code and try to work out, by examining code features, whether there are any security vulnerabilities. Scanners are big business. But realistically, all the scanners do fairly similar things, some have better success in some areas than others. But scanning your code is necessary because secure software development is an utter failure, as it currently stands. Every day there are dozens of critical and high-risk software bugs being discovered. The thing is absolutely full of holes. Even through the vast amount of effort and thinking that has gone into selling vulnerability detection. The vulnerabilities keep appearing. No-one looks to be getting a lasting handle on it.

Bug bounties pay hackers to break into online systems. They are usually paid for the vulnerabilities they discover. This has become an industry. Some might call it a 'racket'. Reading the Nicole Perlroth book "This is how they tell me the world ends", gives a gentle but disturbing introduction into how finding unauthorised access to technology has been perpetuated and monetised at the expense of civilisation.

But also, having tried bug bounties recently, after spending £500 of my own money on security software, I was disappointed that as a relative beginner, there were no real starter websites to try and develop my learning on. Most of the participants in the public campaigns were a few hundred very, very secure web applications. My skills are not great, but also not terrible. Of course, the handful of elite hackers were able to find enough obscure vulnerabilities in them, to pay themselves a handsome sum every month. But nothing for the beginners it seems. This is not a criticism, more to do with my feelings of self-potential and loss. There are around 600 million websites in the world. There are a few hundred of them on HackerOne public listing. For any criticism you might think I was making, HackerOne is a great idea and really useful to facilitate the relationship between hackers, committed to doing good and companies who also would like to improve their security hardness. Keep up the good work. Just need to bring in the other 600 million websites. I am sure there a few that this beginner could help with.

Red teaming is a way of exploring specific threats within an organisation. Instead of just randomly scanning equipment, to see if it is patched. Or trying to break in where you can find holes. Instead, the Red Team is given a task and proceeds to act on objectives. In the same way that an advanced threat actor group would attempt to do something, that has real-world outcomes. For example, the Red Team might work for a Steel Company, and they could try and brick a steel furnace, by switching it off mid-process. Leaving the multi-million-dollar furnace unable to be used again and taking millions to have it deconstructed and removed.

They would probably want to do a tabletop simulation, instead of doing this as a test. Yes, they would probably just simulate it, instead of actually doing it. But there are other examples of real-world objectives that Red Teams could do that would not have lasting impacts. But you also want to test things that have a lasting impact. ost of the HackerOne bug bounties stipulate that denial of service is not allowed. This has created a world in which denial of service has never been tested. I am not talking about rate-based network volume type of denial of service. But the type of DoS exploits that crash application processes, redirects data into memory intensive processes, launching database freezes, that sort of thing. None of that is actually being tested. Because companies do not want momentary outages affecting their customers. Which also makes sense. Devops teams use the adage "Move fast and break things". Okay, not that thing!

11 PRINCIPLES IN PRACTICE

IMPORTANT! The hardware browser example given here is for educational purposes. It is not a pattern or design that can be used as a product. Woe betide anyone who takes this and makes people use it for their day job. Without first making it very user friendly. You have been warned!

Principles translate into design features
So far, we have been looking at some principles of IT security which are high level ideas. It is all well having theoretical ideas and concepts. But when you want to actually fix something up in the real world. You need something more tangible, and this is where we go from theory to practice. We will rarely talk about these principles in generic terms. I have often heard service managers talk about role-based access and least privilege principle. But really what they mean is the 'Users & Groups' webpage that is on their marketing website.

Role based access could also be implemented through a more technical thing, like online federated access provider, or an LDAP (Active Directory) service. The concept always has to manifest itself in some tangible piece of technology, with product features and marketing jargon. The reason for talking so much about security principles in the book up to this point is to make it clear that in theory, there are relatively few categories of security controls, when you strip away all the jargon and marketing spin. And most of the ideas have been around since pre-history, with their implementations taking various forms throughout the ages. We can take the ideas and re-apply them to the future.

Securing the core components
Digital IT systems enhance our lives in all sorts of ways. They are sometimes vast and very complex. Containing tens of thousands of components in some cases. But at the core of each design there are a probably just a half a dozen technology types, such as a webserver, an operating system, network drivers, an application framework, a cloud hypervisor, some IoT device, or a database. For this example, I have chosen to illustrate a browser design, not because the browser is the least secure component in any current system. In fact, it is considered to be one of the most secure components. But it is not hackproof. There are many vulnerabilities revealed for the browsers on the market every year and any one of them could allow those rich enough to buy those exploits and the technocrats who manage to find them, full access to any browser they can capture. Of course, once you start using an exploit it starts to get discovered, so those who pay a lot of money for exploits have to be careful how they use them. We have already seen how honeypots and honey monkey browsers are used to find exploits.

The main ways that a browser gets hacked
Referring to the extensive library of previously disclosed vulnerabilities in the very excellent and long-standing compendium that is exploitdb. Looking at real exploits that exist for the Opera browser, there are a range of issues, including overflows - heap, stack and integer. Command and code execution bugs. Plus, a lot of denial-of-service exploits, that the researcher could not find a reliable Remote Code Execution (RCE) exploit for. But an RCE could still exist.

Principles in Practice   155

There are very many more, for other browsers, including Chrome, Chromium, Safari, Edge and Firefox.

```
Opera Browser 10.60 - Clickjacking
Opera Browser 10/11/12 - 'SVG Layout' Memory Corruption (Met
Opera Browser 6.0 6 - URI Display Obfuscation
Opera Web Browser 10.01 - 'dtoa()' Remote Code Execution
Opera Web Browser 11.00 - 'option' HTML Element Integer Over
Opera Web Browser 11.00 - Integer Overflow
Opera Web Browser 11.11 - Denial of Service
Opera Web Browser 11.11 - Remote Crash
Opera Web Browser 11.52 - Escape Sequence Stack Buffer Overf
Opera Web Browser 12.11 - Crash (PoC)
Opera Web Browser 7 - IFRAME Zone Restriction Bypass
Opera Web Browser 7.0 - Remote IFRAME Denial of Service
Opera Web Browser 7.23 - Empty Embedded Object JavaScript De
Opera Web Browser 7.23 - JavaScript Denial of Service
Opera Web Browser 7.5 - Resource Detection
Opera Web Browser 7.53 - Location Replace URI Obfuscation
Opera Web Browser 7.54 - 'KDE KFMCLIENT' Remote Command Exec
Opera Web Browser 7.54 java implementation - Multiple Vulner
Opera Web Browser 7.54 java implementation - Multiple Vulner
Opera Web Browser 7.54 java implementation - Multiple Vulner
Opera Web Browser 7.54 java implementation - Multiple Vulner
Opera Web Browser 7.5x - IFrame OnLoad Address Bar URL Obfus
Opera Web Browser 7.x - URI Handler Directory Traversal
Opera Web Browser 8.0/8.5 - HTML Form Status Bar Misrepresen
Opera Web Browser 8.51 - URI redirection Remote Code Executi
Opera Web Browser 8.52 - Stylesheet Attribute Buffer Overflo
Opera Web Browser 9 - CSS Background URI Memory Corruption
Opera Web Browser 9.00 - 'iframe' Remote Denial of Service
Opera Web Browser 9.26 - Multiple Vulnerabilities
Opera Web Browser 9.62 - History Search Input Validation
Opera Web Browser 9.x - History Search and Links Panel Cross
Opera Web Browser < 11.60 - Denial of Service / Multiple Vul
```

These attacks target the browser application software, usually when it processes some web content by visiting a malicious website. The content causes the web browser software to glitch. Sometimes causing a memory overflow, into a region of memory that causes the software to break, a denial of service. Sometimes the hacker manages to find a way of further exploiting the memory bug to find a remote code execution, that allows them to run arbitrary code within the browser process. Some exploits will allow the hacker to run code that is provided as an input to a function.

Take for example the exploit in the list about, third from the top, called 'dtoa()' Remote Code Execution. The exploit code looks like this:

```
<script>
var a=0.<?php echo str_repeat("1",296450); ?>;
</script>
```

Those who are malware experts will want to comment. But this exploit works by abusing the binary decimal to floating point conversion routine dtoa() by assigning the variable 'a' with a 0.1111111...[recursion]. Appending a very long series of ones after the decimal point. When the browser loads the JavaScript and tries to assign the value, it will cause the browser to crash, if the hacker is able to work up an exploit, they could insert their own code at the right location and the flow of execution might run it. The user might not even notice anything has happened. If they can conveniently exit back into the running program. The hacker then has exploit code running within the context of the running process. But that does not give them much in a modern browser.

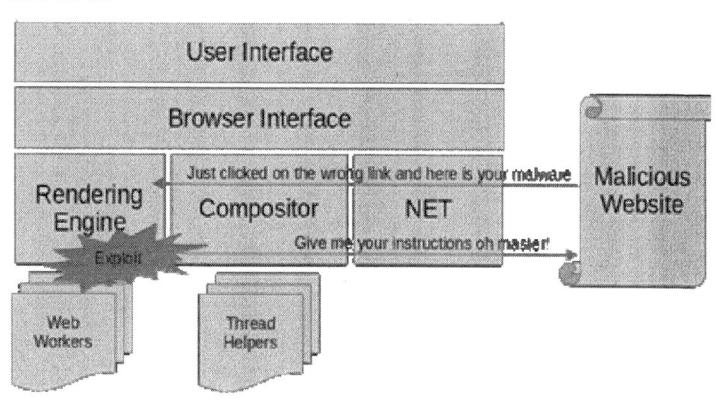

Chromium and Chrome were possibly the first browsers to implement per tab sandboxing. So the hacker code in theory, will not be able to interact with any other tabs. Nor

Principles in Practice

will it be able to escape into the device, that is running the browser and look at files on the mobile operating system, or laptop hard drive. The exploit code, browser trojans, such as Zeus and Qbot, should be contained within the sandbox. But there are sandbox escapes and variants that sometimes appear that use them. It is an arms race between the browser features and the malware features.

Attacking the browser itself is quite an extreme sort of attack. Usually the reserve of elite hackers, known as Advanced Persistent Threat (APT) actors. There is a list of them on the very excellent MITRE Attack website. These could be super-villains, military cyberwar units, or mercenary groups. That have seemingly unlimited resources and time to work on their skills and tools. But when considering browser weaknesses, the browser software is not the low hanging fruit.

There are also a range of web application attacks that can be enabled by the browser, that have nothing to do with weaknesses in its core application code. Having recently completed a web application testing course, over the space of several months. You might ask why a 54-year-old family man, would retrain to be an ethical hacker. Yes, I am not sure either and I have put the idea on hold. But if you are interested and have a strong moral compass, search for portswigger[dot]net for their free learning materials.

With the current state of web application security, most of the attacks do not need any help from browser bugs that attack the browser application processes. There are plenty of vulnerabilities already available that run on top of the browser and the browser mostly facilitates the client-side aspect of attacks, without it being considered a security fault. Built-in browser functionality, such as CORS, autocomplete, DOM interactions with JavaScript content, HTTP proxy cache, and web sockets between origins. Just to name a few. These are all considered normal functionality of the browser and exist for the sake of performance and usability. The browser co-operates with the attacker, based on a loose workable arrangement, where the browser has to respond in universally predictable ways. That the hacker then uses as the basis for their attack.

Of course, it is possible to modify and recompile the browser to remove all the unwanted functionality. But the browser, content delivery, servers and applications all make up an interoperability ecosystem. Changing one aspect of it, can have impact on the rest. Do not think that building a secure browser will do anything other than annoying a lot of people, unless it can be refined to a high art and becomes fully functional and interoperable with the rest of global web technologies.

But going back to the reason why we are even considering this exercise. There are core components of IT systems, and the browser is considered one of the most secure. A fully patched browser software should be considered secure because the zero-day exploits will not likely fall into the hands of enough low-level threat actors to threaten you as a user. Unless you are a spy, a military dictator, or a human rights activist. The diagram a couple of pages back, shows the way that the browser would be hacked by a hardcore remote code execution memory bug. Like one of the many zero-day exploits that have appeared in browsers during 2023. The diagram is simplistic and for illustration only.

"Hackproof" vs. "secure enough" browser

It took me a number of years and several failed software projects, to discover that there is a marked difference between an invention and a product that satisfies a business proposition. It is the difference between making a go-cart, buying a new car, taking a taxi, or investing in a driverless chauffeur service. These are all based on the invention of a cart with four wheels that resembles what we think of as a car. But it will not help me if I have to get from Reading to Holborn in two hours. What I need is something that ticks all the boxes. If you have ever commuted into London regularly, as I have, you will know that there are several reasons why you would always prefer the train and the underground. But for convenience here, let's say that you would easily prefer the driverless over the taxi and probably more than driving your own car. But more than breaking the law by driving a motorised go-cart along the M4 motorway. Needless to say, there are a whole bunch of factors that make up a convincing business proposition. The worked example here is an invention, it may not even work when you try it. It certainly will not work as a business proposition, so do not try to sell it as a product please! It is a go-cart, not a taxi.

Looking for a business proposition that would enable a new type of hackproof browser to enter the market. For one thing you would be competing with one of the most powerful tech companies in the world, who own 60-70% of the market. And for good reason, because the Chrome browser is very usable and mostly secure. It is just not hackproof. There were fourteen known and published zero-day exploits in the top browser in 2023. That means that any point in the last few years, any one of those vulnerabilities could have been used. That does not mean the bar was low. There are very clever hackers out there, who can find bugs at will. There are also many very rich patrons who are willing to pay top dollar for those exploits. It is an exclusive "access all areas" type of club. That brings out something of a socialist in me that I never knew was there. The effectiveness of browser patching has increased in my perception over the past few years and auto-updates will have made most of the zero-days unusable within a short span of them being discovered. So, for the average user, this is a no-brainer. The browser is certainly secure enough – it has good enough security for almost all uses.

What is the issue then? For the large corporation, handling billions in financial transactions, medical research centres making new drugs that everyone will use, military leaders and politicians using web applications to plan wars and elections. All these still use the same browser, do not be deceived. It is the best we can expect, given a range of received design prerequisites. Early in the competition for the browser market, the European Union produced their own browser, the information provided with it appeared to be hopeful. But within a few years it was no longer supported. There were a series of bugs discovered and I think the support team just decided not to continue. The same appears to be the case with the many other browsers that have contended for mainstream adoption over the years. There is a Wikipedia diagram entitled "Timeline_of_web_browsers" that shows the progression of browser technologies. With the main technical implementation in green focussed around the Webkit/Blink rendering engine used by Chrome and Chromium. But even though there are many timelines reaching the present, on the right-hand side of the diagram. Proportionally, Chrome is the outstanding market winner https://en.wikipedia.org/wiki/Usage_share_of_web_browsers, with StatCounter desktop figures for 2023, showing Chrome at 66%, Safari at 19%, Edge at 4% and Firefox now at just 3%. With the mobile figures similarly distributed.

It is inconceivable that even with the prospect of an average user being robbed of a large percentage of their income every year, that they would a) attribute any loss to their choice of leading browser, b) make any investigation into whether they could improve the situation. It is a market forces fix, that has already made that decision, for the majority of the world's population. A simple equation of supply and demand. The majority do not need another solution.

Strangely, with the exception of around 600 million KaiOS users in India. KaiOS is based on the Firefox operating system and runs on inexpensive flip phones, from the likes the Alcatel, Motorola and Nokia. It has taken the lion's share of the Indian market, and the assumption would be that it uses the Firefox (Gecko) browser but I am not sure that is correct. KaiOS is able to use a multitude of software similar to Android and iPhone and there is a burgeoning market for its apps. I am fairly sure it will run Chrome and most users probably do (big assumption). So, there are exceptions and the main business proposition here is that a KaiOS phone will probably cost ten times less than most phones in Europe and North America. Which could be proportional to Indian wages. KaiOS follows on the tail of Symbian, which used to be the main mobile operating system before Android. It has a similar small resolution interface and icons. I would hazard to say that unfortunately KaiOS will not solve all the worlds mobile security issue. Maybe they will. I would like to hear that discussion.

The business proposition for a new type of hackproof browser would need to be seamlessly interoperable with existing websites. Be able to function with web technologies in the background in a similar way. It would need to be easily installable and without any licensing issues. Of course, it would be free. But more than any of this, it would need to be more impressive in performance than Chrome and take the world's media by storm. This is the pure power aspect, and it is less likely to happen than oil disappearing from the stock markets in 2024. Don't get me wrong, there is nothing on a daily basis that troubles me with using Chrome. Apart from the world is being hacked to pieces in so many different ways and at the centre of the chaos is a small number of expansively used technologies. I am writing this book on my Ubuntu laptop, with LibreOffice and Brave browser, in case you were wondering. But under my desk is a Windows 10 workstation, with Chrome installed. You do not have to go far to come across the most popular software. I have sometimes heard people say that they would not go in a driverless car, but then they go out and drive on the same road as the driverless cars. Ultimate security goals need a systemic solution.

Perhaps if hackproof browser inventions did make it to the product stage, there could be a niche market for high end Privileged Access Workstations (PAW), which is the recommendation by some governments for the most sensitive critical infrastructure clients. There was a similar market for Citrix and Wyse terminals when there was propositional value in thin client access, as a form of security control. This is still used in some cases. But it is clear from many published research papers that thin client is generally ineffective at preventing a number of attacks that it was used to prevent, prior to around 2010. Occasionally, I still come across it as a proposed mitigation. But there are lots of openly available tools to tunnel through Citrix and RDS client sessions from the victim desktop. The access end of the thin client needs to be secure, for its overall use to be secure.

Most developers would agree that your standard browsers, Chrome/Chromium, Safari, Firefox, Edge, Opera and Brave are secure. You do not need to do anything additionally with them. I am not sure where this idea came from. Take as an example the various HoneyMonkey, or Browser Honeypot projects that are out there. They use standard browser technology with additional code, or scripting, to deliberately get the browser compromised and then analyse how the exploit works. It is used by security researchers, to understand what malware is currently being used on the internet. Apparently, it does not take long to find some content that will compromise the browser somehow.

Companies will very often use a web filtering gateway to browse the internet and a website categorisation service to barre unwanted website types. This approach is usually found with larger companies and public sector organisations. It offers some additional protection and often downloaded files and web content can also be scanned for malware. The effectiveness of its malware prevention abilities is rarely questioned, and any independent market research tends to be expensive and commissioned by large companies for in-house use only. Also, browsers integrate with a desktop operating system, mobile phone, television, or tablet. The way in which the operating system interacts with the browser is also a factor. You may receive a link through a messaging app, you click on the link and the browser opens.

Also scripting, mostly JavaScript and Typescript, is the feature that has really opened up the browser experience over the past ten years. Without scripting support, the web would not be as useful as we know it. This is a difficult dilemma from a security point of view, and many extensions and features have been added to scripting libraries to try to reduce the risk posed by scripting. Such as the httpOnly browser setting that is implemented as an HTTP header value. When the website sets a cookie (session token), the httpOnly header only allows session tokens to be sent in HTTP requests, when associated with user action and not through JavaScript as a code decision only. But having spent several months in the last year, studying the latest web application hacking skills with Portswigger.net, it has become clear that the httpOnly header is not massively effective in a lot of cases. Our worked example will need to mitigate the threat of arbitrary scripting and request redirection. As this can be a minefield of security mistakes. But it also means if we keep scripting, there is a risk of malware. If we lose the scripting, the user experience is going to be very limited.

Why choose to implement in electronics, rather than software? The rationale for this, going back to the principles is firstly for safekeeping. About a year or two ago, there were a number of laptop issues, with manufacturers of corporate laptops. The TPM chip on a laptop motherboard, is an encryption key safe for launching Bitlocker drive encryption at boot-time. The keys needed to unlock the encrypted drive image are stored in the secure TPM module, means that the business user does not need to enter a boot pin, when they power up the laptop. But researchers have found that in some cases, using a logic analyser probe, a standard bit of electronics kit, I have one in my electronics lab at home. It has little claws that you can clip onto the legs of a silicon chip. Using the probe, the researchers could intercept the encryption keys, on the SPI comms bus of the motherboard, between the TPM and the processor. It takes some special decoding with software, but the keys are visible in the clear. There is a level of technical ability involved but a range of laptops were susceptible. Any of them that were using Bitlocker with TPM keys could be opened if they could find a skilled local criminal and my guess is there are probably many of them. Up to that point, TPM key storage was a great user experience feature. That allowed disks to be encrypted but without the user having to remember a pin. Since then, I think the laptop manufacturers have put out mostly new fixes for the TPM issue. But that is a good reason to start the hackproof aspirational requirements with electronics, rather than software.

When looking at the number of attacks against browsers as they are at the moment. The hacks tend to work at the web application layer and are based on the features of the target website mostly. But there is still some potential for exploitation of the browser. Exploits that affect the user data, the integration with desktop and extensions, plus the high-end sandbox escapes (and tab escapes). Web hacks and sandbox escapes are still an issue. But most ransomware episodes start more simply with users clicking on the wrong link and being fooled into typing their credentials into the wrong web interface. This is more of a user decision making issue. But there are technical factors that make it far more likely, and this can also be addressed in our worked example.

The primary need for security constraints in IT system design

[This part is a little technical, but you can do an internet search if you are interested.] Since the start of computing, the design process has been focused on the primary use case and not on

security. When I am developing software to do something, generally I am not thinking about security. It will come either built in, and I don't have to think about it. Or it is an afterthought if there is any requirement for security. In a lot of personal development projects, there is no need for security as the software will never be used to host confidential production systems used in business and government. In chapter 2, I mentioned the difference between microprocessors, multi-processor, versus monoprocessor (embedded) and how some applications use ASICs because it is more efficient. It also means that the computer is not general use and will not run any old code. It will only run the code it was designed to. Which severely restrict the potential for compromise. There are exceptions, if input is able to be manipulated somehow. Also, the use of libc gadgets, (search ROP gadgets) allows a hacker to build a new program out of component parts available in libc and jump about between the instructions that are needed. Libc is used in nearly every application you can think of that runs on Linux. The primary requirement for hackproof, I think is to move from general purpose computing to task specific electronics. This is not a great business proposition, but I cannot see the situation improving unless it happens. Using technology like ASICs means that libc and processor instructions are no longer needed because everything is implemented as a gate array using digital logic in hardware.

Reducing dependencies and functionality

Most software containers run on a Debian OS base with dependencies on top (technical - search Docker Hub), which could be node.js, python, java, rust, or ruby – to name some coding language examples. To reduce the footprint even further some containers, replace Debian with Alpine Linux, which is only 5MB in size and uses busybox and Musl libc, as useful dependencies. A dependency is a library or process that the software needs in order to run. One research team recently created a set of "sparse" container images, that allow developers to run executable code, without supporting operating system within the container. But the container still requires an external runtime, whether that is containerd, or CRIO, or another type of shim. Granted that the runtime is a very small OS-like code, necessary to run the container. But it also requires Docker Engine, or some other interpreter/orchestration layer to run all the containers and an underlying host operating system under that. That is a lot of dependencies and layers where potentially bad stuff could happen. Recent attacks against container environments have been using features of the orchestration API, to delete, relocate and then hijack the supervisory functionality within the node, in order to take over the cluster. All of these layers are required to co-ordinate large scale container deployments. It is hard to see where a balance can be struck between the complexity required to orchestrate and the reduction in complexity required to be secure. This is an ongoing struggle in 2024. Going back to our example here. The main whack of security overhaul will be looking at the design of the browser mechanisms and then applying the principles as design requirements.

Turning the principles into hackproof browser design constraints

When thinking about the principles, it develops a mindset that can then be applied to a system or component design. Going from theory to practice is not easy. It is sometimes easier to think, how can I make this as secure as possible and then in retrospect realise that you were just applying a security principle without thinking about it. You learn the principles inside out and then do what comes naturally. Applying the security principles already discussed in the book, manifests itself as a number of design constraints for this hardware browser:

Principle	Design Constraint
Enforcement Point	Avoid arbitrary code execution
Dedicated use	Each component does just one thing
Input Validation	Prefer analogue over digital and hardware over software
Enforcement Point	Disrupt process thoroughfares
Isolation	Physical isolation, avoid buses and pooled resources
Least Functionality	Implement minimal, forego operating systems, tools, drivers and excessive dependencies
Window of Opportunity	Limit the scope of execution, processes run quickly then terminate
Known Good State	Close on failure and quickly reset
Enforcement Point	Manual human input and activation
Data Durability	Write-once read-once data
Enforcement Point	No system components should be networked except the gatekeeper
Logic issues	One way data flow
Statefulness of programs	Design around fixed secure states
Safekeeping Principle	Positive tamper detection

A worked example of a "hackproof" hardware browser

Below is a photo of my workshop bench with equipment from the first attempt that I had at implementing the hardware browser. Needless to say, I did not get enough spare time to work it up to become a fully working prototype. Let alone a product of any description. Let's just say it remains a curiosity in a drawer. Among many others in my electronics lab.

168   Hackproof in Eight Principles

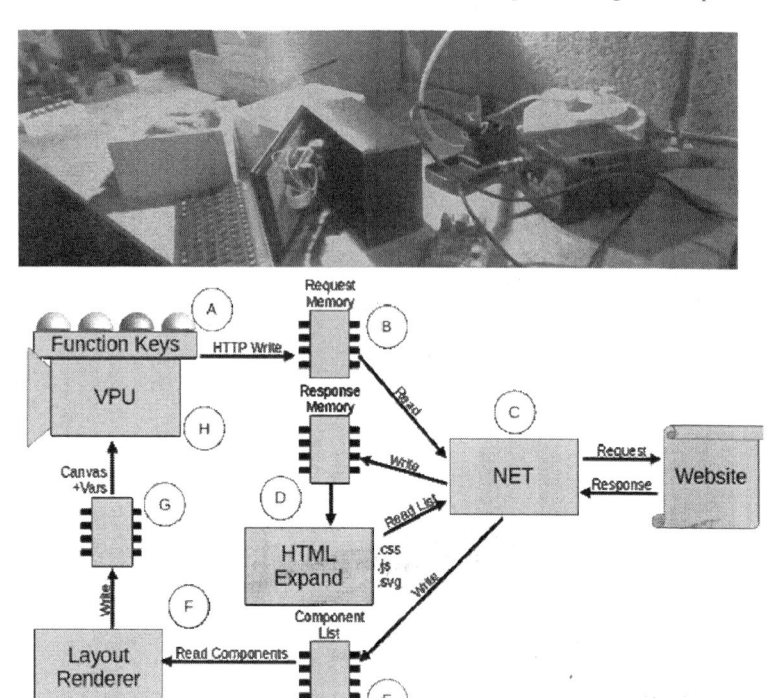

[Diagram: Process flow showing Function Keys, VPU, Request Memory, Response Memory, NET, Website, HTML Expand (.css .js .svg), Component List, Layout Renderer, Canvas+Vars, with labeled nodes A–H and connections labeled HTTP Write, Read, Write, Read List, Read Components, Request, Response, Write.]

This is where it gets really practical. The above diagram is sort of hand drawn. Like all the best innovation diagrams, they started out being drawn on a napkin in a diner, or on the back of a cigarette packet and shown to other like-minded engineers, who know that appearance is not everything. You may mock or criticise and you would be right to do so. But you are now part of the design process. Having studied computer systems at degree level, I should be capable of more. But this is what we have to work with. It is just an illustration. You can try out your own ideas, based on the inspirations in this book.

Description of the process flow:

A) The user input is through a standard keyboard, with additional hardwired function keys. I will get to what those are used for in a minute. The user views the webpages through a standard monitor interface with drivers. This choice was necessary, otherwise you would need to custom built video hardware and software. Not a good idea. In this case, I used Raspberry Pi for the visual processing (VPU) and RPi LCD Display cape for the monitor. But you could use a number of approaches. When the user views the webpage, they are able to type into text fields and press the big red Commit button. Which sends an HTTP network request.

B) The request to the website (HTTP POST or GET request) is written from the VPU to a memory register. In my design I used a 24LC512 serial erasable EEPROM. But you could use any type of memory chip you have available, that you can read and write to. The whole point is having an enforcement point of physical isolation, to avoid process thoroughfares. The write cannot happen without an electronic signal from the big red Commit function key. It is not software driven, so sending out on the network, cannot be bypassed through software. I managed to read and write ascii string values to memory.

C) The networking processor component (NET), is a separate miniature microcontroller. Most likely a ESP32 or similar. You can buy five of them for around $15 in some places. It has no user mode functionality, nor anything really, apart from network drivers, DHCP and DNS clients. It polls the memory in B looking to read any new requests. It then sends the request to the appropriate website location and receives a response. At this point we reach our first difficulty. Websites are not made up of just one component but many. The initial call to retrieve an HTML page will expand into dozens of other necessary page components, such as cascading style sheets (CSS) that define page layout, JavaScript that provides all sorts of page items, interactive content, animations, user functionality and of course images (.gif, .png, .svg).

D) Following our one-way street idea, the initial HTML page is written to another memory chip and then read by yet another small microcontroller, that expands on the requests in the page to retrieve a number of other page components. The microcontroller requests the page content.

E) The whole list of page content is written as files to yet another separate memory chip (would have to be bigger than 512k this time) and waits to be read by the layout renderer.

F) The layout renderer would need to be a standard Chromium renderer, or Gecko, or Webkit. At this point you might be saying, well isn't that just the same as a regular software browser. After some thought, I decided to make a concession and yes it would be better to implement it in some even more strict hardware design. But in order to add value without re-inventing the wheel, this will drastically improve the potential for malware to control the browser. Preventing it from steal credentials or data, and any number of other issues to do with the security of the browser. It does not solve clicking on the wrong link, or some website design issues that cause request redirection. But the malware problem has gone away. The execution window of opportunity is reduced. There is no way to make requests programmatically, the access to the network from the renderer is gated through separate hardware and human physical activation.

G) In the last stage. The renderer screenshots the browser window in memory and writes an image file of the webpage, adding variable slots into the memory. This is pulled in (read) by the VPU which renders the display image to the screen using an X virtual frame buffer. I got this bit to work. The second major issue is that although the JavaScript meant for layout is effective, the JavaScript used to interact with the user will not work. So in effect, this will break the majority of websites and things like social media, that do not offer a NoScript alternative to things like password entry. You would need to use a retrospective Web 1.0 webserver for this to work and that severely limits the use cases for business and personal use.

H) The image on the display has a number of slots

defined that contain an overlay to enter text parameter entries, such as name, address, telephone, etc. The user selects the slot using a function button and can retrieve bookmarks, tokens, or stored values (not shown) from a local cache. To write to the disk requires manual button press (hard IRQ). This is the most likely part to be hacked and probably needs more work. But you get the idea. Press the Commit button again and the form with the data is submitted and you go back to step A again.

This is a very rudimentary design, used purely for illustrative purposes. There are better ways of doing all of this and that is why system development is still a well-paid job. The point is to understand that security principles and ideas can manifest themselves in design features, at every level. They do not have to be a casual afterthought but can be included in the design process, at a low level they become effective in changing the whole IT security narrative.

12 CONCLUSIONS

Change is inevitable
The whole point of this book is considering the security ideology of IT - past, present and future. Although I am no Dickens, I hope that I have inspired you and given you hope, that the future can be different. It has helped me to stop and think about what is going on. Thirty years is a long time to be thinking about computer networks and security. This is going to make me sound ancient and out of touch with the latest tech but bear with me because there is a point.

In 1996, when I worked as a junior at Citibank, I was involved in the replacement of network technology that had been used for about ten years, that was made up of 10Base2 Ethernet. We were starting to install twisted pair ethernet with RJ45, the network cabling that we know today. I know everyone uses Wi-Fi now. With the coax, you would lay a terminated hundred and eighty metres of coaxial cable, similar to a television antenna. Then add intrusive, or non-intrusive taps into the length of cable. Each cable would have maybe two dozen computers on it. The desktop computers would be attached to the taps (small boxes).

The lengths of coax would be plugged into a switch using bayonet connectors, that you push and twist. All the switches would be connected together over the floors in the building using a collapsed fibre backbone, that used the FDDI protocol. That was similar to Ethernet but is no longer used now.

When I connected my network management laptop (one of the first of its kind) to the network, I cannot remember having to enter a password on the laptop, it was before passwords on personal devices. All the management software was on the laptop, there were no internal websites. It could scan around the whole network, without any restrictions and most of the network equipment used SNMP version 1, that did not require a "*community string*" (password) to get access to everything. It was all like that at the start of cyber history.

Of course, you would need strong doors on the server room and if you logged into the local terminal, it would need a password. After all it was a bank. But security was extreme in the physical world but less so in cyberspace, during that moment in time. We managed firewalls and hardware encryptors but nothing like the advanced technologies we have today. Citibank were one of the first organisations to appoint a CISO and when I first heard about it, they explained his position to me, as if he was actually an agency, like the FBI or the men in black. "They all carry guns you know". Which as a man in his late twenties inspired a fantasy or two. The reality was probably more like we know a CISO today but without the present confidence. We had no idea at that time what was coming over the hill.

There was no need for more advanced network security controls, as the hacker revolution had not really started in the minds of businesspeople. Fast forward twenty-five years and this all sounds ludicrous. Like some strange dream, where everything is the same but slightly different. My point is that the past appears to be the same but different. The future will be the same but different.

We can make the changes that are needed to meet the threats of the future, to conceptualise the way it could be and open up different ways of doing things. Back in 1996, the main thing that was missing, apart from not being able to get twisted pair cabling and ethernet switches deployed fast enough. Were the ideas that I describe in this book, that have mostly been around since pre-history, that are now applied to the security context we find ourselves in. You could apply them to the future.

How could we use the security ideas?

The next big disruptive change in the cyber security world could come from a brand-new concept, that has never been thought of before. But as I mentioned a moment ago, most of these security ideas have been around for a very long time and they are often rebooted in slightly different ways but make a massive difference. Here is the list of concepts from earlier chapters in this book. We could consider how these principles can be applied. I have offered some suggestions. Feel free to write in the margins, if you have the paper version.

Trusted person – for a long time, countries have been trying to implement national identity databases, some smaller European countries have achieved it. The inability to opt out, means that there is theoretically a complete view of the nation's population. But the human rights lobby, is quick to identify some countries, as not being suitable to have a greater handle on their population, than they do already. A lot of the re-identification of online personas, is intertwined with political advocacy and the same ability to expose cyber criminals, may unwittingly expose those vulnerable to political threats of violence, and oppression. As mentioned below, AI video interviews, such as those used in recruitment by companies like Hirevue, that have received a number of different criticisms, and yet appear to be taking a large portion of the online recruitment market. Having to align with recent AI legislation. It may be that services like these will eventually extend into general HR interviews. Like the system checks from the film Blade Runner. Humans in positions of responsibility may need to check in with an artificial security officer, who acutely understands what creates trust and loyalty within their organisation and is trained to catch out those who are trying to fool the system. This may have a counter effect on big tech's influence within organisations, as loyalty to suppliers is by definition fraud. Technology has created a web of counter-tensions, that are straining as we turn the corners of history. There is no way of putting these things back in the box.

With the safekeeping principles we could find ourselves in this sort of position. You have a financial payments team that want to transfer a large amount of money to a new vendor. The vendor has been setup in the procurement system and all the due diligence checks have been done. As well as using the separation of duties checks that have been severely defeated in recent years, there is also an AI behavioural baseline that checks recent online activity and may also intervene and ask some questions in a popup. To train the AI, you need to train a language-based classifier on what a criminal would say and what a non-criminal would say. So, you go to a prison and locate criminals to help train the AI. They are willing for cash to help you and are not able to pretend to be non-criminals enough, to change the outcome. You have what you want from the criminal training set. But what about the non-criminals? How do you clearly identify non-criminals? So now we are the anti-police and are out to identify and catch non-criminals. They could be recently retired manual workers on modest pension. Probably not destitute because surely crime does not pay. The super-rich well they will get a call. How about children, but yes they could be pre-criminal children. Using polygraph testing might give us some leverage with our candidate. You can see my point. At every stage there is a potential for staff being wrongly accused and payments not going through. At the moment in the UK there is a Financial Services

Compensation Scheme (FSCS) that will refund you up to $85,000 (£85,000 or €85,000) as a citizen, if you lose money to a cybercrime online. I guess the thinking behind that is "why not be wronged" and just absorb the loss. The same goes for shoplifting. But there comes a point where shoplifting becomes all out looting and the absorption effect takes everything you have. We may be approaching that at some point, I do not have those figures.

Confirmed identity – Service Principal Authorizations is a fairly dry term and probably needs unpacking a little bit. Going back to the safekeeping principles and trusted person. An actual human being becomes a trusted person through reliable shared experience over a long period of time. Or it can be more basic, like a formal background check. That they move into the realms of confirmed identity and making sure they are who they say they are, like a passport or some other photo ID. Once the person is trusted and their identity is confirmed, they can be assigned some privileges, like authorization to access the cleaning closet, or use power tools in an office. That usually gets aligned with the job that they do for the organisation. But when an application running on some system has been given rights and permissions to access certain databases, or process input from filing system. Then the application is generically called a "service principle" and it has a set of authorizations. Now we understand that a bit. Let's move on to how that has progressed in the past few years. A lot of applications and online SaaS websites now have the ability to install add-ins. These are the aftermarket plugin components that other companies produce to give a little bit of their functionality in your supplier's application. I could go and make a list but I think it would become commercially ridiculous. So, let's say you search online for data analytics and Customer Resource Management (CRM), it's probably those lot. Add-ins have also now crossed over into management platforms a lot more and devops teams are keen to consolidate their tools into a single pane of glass view and that is understandable (and possibly lazy? You know who you are!). One of the main exponents of service principal overloading is the messaging client. You can now configure your favourite messaging application to do all sorts of things it was never intended to do. This completely overloads the least functionality principle. But the risk/advantage benefits are so outweighed at the moment, especially with AI assistants also being added. Companies are deciding to put all their application control into a messaging desktop client application, instead of a more secure browser. Over time, this may have a more dramatic effect in continuing the phishing effect that we have been experiencing with email for the past twenty years.

Physical security – depending on how safe the world is, data centres are a more, or less safe place to store data. In some countries, it is only really safe in underground bunkers whose identity is not widely known. The centralising effect of just a handful of cloud service providers managing all online IT, may lead to some backlash where covert hidden hosting becomes a trend. It is more likely that CSPs will take full control of the IT market and data centres will become fortresses.

With the increase in IoT products, tamperproof technologies may become more necessary, as a security measure. As we have seen with the Payment Card Industry, Pin Entry Devices (PED) that you put your card into at the supermarket. Most of them now have strong tamperproof features and process checks to ensure that they have not been broken into. The same might happen with IoT devices although they are designed in a domestic setting to blend into the background. In industrial, medical and agricultural settings, and as part of distributions chains. These tamperproof checks may become more necessary. Using techniques similar to bank notes, introducing swirling patterns and special materials that humans can detect flaws in but criminals find hard to rectify or imitate.

Known good state – some systems refresh their infrastructure and application every week, this is becoming more of a feature of contemporary cloud deployments and something that should be encouraged. With traditional servers, if you experienced a major fault and had to rebuild everything, in a lot of cases it would take weeks to do. Now with the use of Terraform and Blue/Green deployment, it is possible to refresh configuration and reset the system to a known good state on a more frequent basis. Which means if there has been some compromise, it is less likely to endure.

Hardening – recent moves away from monolithic operating system-based servers or virtual machines to a more compact, container or serverless approach to IT. Has meant that focus on reducing the available attack surface, so the hacker has nothing to try and subvert. This has gained some traction recently. In fact, it has meant that some organisations have preferred the reduction in functionality, to the addition of extra security tooling. The security tool manufacturers have been trying to re-align their products to work with application containers and serverless lambdas. But many of these features are embedded in the cloud service providers platforms and this will require a rethink on the part of many security industry suppliers.

Fearsome reputation - large corporations can sometimes find themselves giving off the wrong vibes and it became clear for some attackers, that they have got themselves into some really deep long-lasting trouble. Take for instance robbers who try to take on the Las Vegas establishment at removing casino funds. Those involved would be well advised to stay well clear of that job and keep an eye over their shoulder for men in dark suits. But the smaller companies, a local engineering firm, a retail shop, a pharmacist, or a car parts company. All of these businesses would struggle to secure their systems and would also not deter criminals without a fearsome reputation. Like the film 'The Magnificent Seven', where a group of mercenary cowboys elect to protect a village of mostly women and children, from a Mexican warlord and his small army. Protecting the little guy is a noble cause but mostly not a careful use of resources. Perhaps at some point, there will be a societal construct that changes this position. It is a poor example but imagine that the internet becomes completely decentralised, each company provides a piece of the backbone infrastructure of the web. Companies could organise themselves in unions, to ban hacker identities from the networks, in a similar way that private precincts co-ordinate shoplifting bans. This is a terrible example, but you get the idea that it might be possible, given a set of disruptive changes, to the way the internet works. Everything can have a secondary effect for security, keep an eye out for opportunities.

Enforcement point - Initial credentials input is another area that is being railroaded with the recent advancements in cloud and desktop features. Windows and other OS desktops used to closely tie credentials input to a secure GINA login interface on the desktop. This would then be integrated with other online services within the organisation. Now we are seeing more frequently with suppliers that they allow customers and general public to enter their credentials directly into a website login page. With large tech companies, their login pages are probably equivalent to the federated access providers and their front-end application security is probably similar level. But smaller startups want to do the same thing and have the same look and feel as the big companies. They are inducing their customers and other to enter credentials into applications that could quite easily be hacked at some point. The same goes with self-managed cloud in large enterprises, it used to be that active directory, or some other third-party security provider would give you a secure page to enter your credentials. All the software mechanisms behind the scenes were hardened and least functionality and also isolated from the target application. Going back to Windows, the GINA login widget was closely tied to the LSASS authentication process and that was a very secure process that was only hacked a couple of times if I remember. It is still a very good choice of access control mechanism. Companies are also waking up to the fact they cannot ask AI to validate a trusted person and confirm their identity and what they should have access to. But maybe one day soon they will be asked to do that. But in the meantime, organisations should be focusing on using hardened access control mechanisms. And not wrapping application access in weak login pages because they think they are like the big tech providers.

Positional advantage - When a user logs into a web application, the front-end of the application, the bit you log into will usually ask for credentials (username and password) or be authorised based on a mobile number, or email address. The back-end database, where the information resides has for a long time used the same authorisation credentials, from the application to the database, the same single username and password, or API string for all users. This has been a common pattern of deployment and having assessed hundreds of well-known suppliers, I can only think of a handful of them where this is not the case. It is not an unacceptable approach, but it is risky. It used to rest on the security of positional advantage. The database was only available to the application. There has been in recent years a move to use back-end APIs that allow individual access control to back-end "on-behalf-of" the front-end user. I think this trend is likely to progress and welcome it as a very effective means of protecting large personal data sets. It is as simple as re-routing front-end requests with OAuth protocol. But it does require additional access processing overhead. OAuth is a feature that a lot of front-end websites already use and not a major uplift compared to the amount of security value it provides. Using a regular database, such as MySQL for a user database has long been frowned upon in favour of a secure access control mechanism like Active Directory but even AD uses the ESE database in the background. In fact, most of the world's secure systems rely on the ESE database which has been around since the 1980s. But it is the positioning, that means that the ESE is only reachable from the secure process that fronts it. No-one is getting to that sucker.

Dedicated use – the increase in IoT and AI products (such as Alexa) may create a situation where more computing devices are dedicated to a single use. Like a necklace with AI chip that is used for language translation. A GPS compass. Cloud electronics for things like dedicated AI models, or in-memory databases. There could be a place for monoprocessors, or sparse container implementations that are only able to run one set of code. It may be possible to intersperse assembler code with keys that can validate each instruction, run on a specific processor, to couple processor to code. Although this sounds like an attractive alternative to creating custom chips. Remember that ASLR memory protection was hacked after five minutes.

Isolation – we have tried physical isolation in lots of ways, and it has only gone to prove that "freedom is going deeper" and not in isolation from others. There is of course, continued value in logical isolation techniques and appropriation. For over a decade, companies have been removing full-trust networks and pooled resources, such as open network shares, within networks that were assumed to

Conclusions

be impenetrable. I think the full-trust aspect of physically isolated systems is now pretty much over.

Obscurity – is one principle which we could probably use more. I remember proposing in early 2000s, to change the Windows directory structure for a whole organisation, to disrupt a well-known malware, from being able to execute. As it relied on certain folders being present for the malware to work. But the difficulty is that you are not able to add extra software to the server because the installation package requires those folders as well. With containers, the applications are all separate, build is all defined in the "dockerfile" and this may provide an opportunity for obscurity to evade some forms of malware.

Applied complexity and exhaustable effort – quantum resistant encryption should be the obvious thing to add here but recommendations from reliable sources this year have told security managers to deprioritise its implementation.

Mathematical certainty – this is one of the least utilised and probably most valuable principles in this list. If we could create some security controls that have mathematical certainty about them, it would be a tremendous breakthrough. To get inspired, read the Simon Singh book "Fermat's Last Theorem". It is a really compelling and well written short history of Mathematics. Focussed on the work of an Oxford mathematician, in reconstructing an equation from 3800 years ago, that was not supposed to exist, but someone had discovered it in the 1630s. They made a note that the proof existed but then no further evidence could be found. Until some further investigation in the 1990s came up with a breakthrough. It makes you believe that anything is possible with mathematics, and it could be that a breakthrough in that subject will change everything for IT security in the future.

Intrigue and trickery – there has to be far more that the defender can do to get one over on the attacker. After all they are in your manor, why would you let them "bust your crib", without a few surprises! Deception technologies have been around for a while now and honeypots and honeytokens are effective ways of threat hunting in among legitimate production systems. There have to be some more "Home Alone" tricks up our sleeves. Spy manuals are full of ways of revealing the mole by running the flags, there should be room for additional tooling that encompasses these kinds of techniques.

Roles and Least privilege – not much to say here. Useful principle that has carried the can for a long time now. Keep up the good work.

Authorized action – the concept of whether actions are permitted at a low level are usually sentinel processes of the operating system, or application. Linking authorized actions to behavioural expectations, rather than have the system check that the password and session token are still confidential. Instead, it may be "not what you know, but who you know", that may eventually take over this thought space. That exists at the centre of IT security. You know your AI assistant. The AI assistant has a strong "community" and humans are on the edge of that community. The village has for many centuries been the definition of an atrium of sanctuary and virtual communities created by AI may be an extension of that idea. With security based on long-term behavioural observations.

Separation of duties – some of the security value we have seen with this in the past few years has come from outsourcing, particularly federated access providers. Creating a Guantanamo enclave, means that it is harder for smooth

Conclusions

talkers to run roughshod over processes and blur the lines by leveraging close working relationships. Cloud service providers running infrastructure have also contributed to orderliness and process rigour. GenAI may create the ideal opportunities for just the right amount of flexibility and personability. Whilst still sticking to access procedures. We will see. At the moment, GenAI is being persuaded to do a lot of things that it does not want to do. GenAI personal assistants may become useful in reinforcing our better selves, at times when we may be feeling susceptible to negative influences. Don't buy it!

Session fixation – token recycling times are starting to be reduced. The access/refresh token scheme means that tokens can only be used once, meaning that if a token is stolen, it cannot be replayed. This is already used a lot with mobile apps and may continue to increase in use and also be used with desktop applications.

Input validation – the use of AI with code generation is currently undergoing a revolution. This could mean that input validation issues will become a thing of the past. Sometimes it is not because the need for input validation has not been identified. But it could be because the developer does not know how to best code the regular expression. Hopefully code assistants will provide the bridge that forums are not able to provide in writing bespoke regex filters.

Logic issues, comprehension and confirmation biases – GenAI is not able to solve the logic issues, and neither can scanning software. But hopefully with AI providing more spare time, the brains of computer scientists can be applied to the complex task of unravelling business logic issues in their software products. Animation is improving and AI generated animation also. It may be possible to visualise complex processes using AI generated animations. Again, something similar. There is still no easy way of viewing the transition between HTTP requests in a website. In a way that allows a security tester to clearly see what is happening. This is one of the contributing factors to continuing poor web security. Some very clever hackers are able to visualise the transitions and carry over all the information in their brains but for the rest of us it would be useful to have some sort of visualisation tools.

Window of opportunity – as I illustrated in the hackproof hardware browser, closing the windows of opportunity in code execution, is as simple as not allowing continued arbitrary code execution from an existing processor.

Statefulness of programs – research in the past year has demonstrated that little is actually known about the true nature of computer statefulness in modern systems. We had a very crude thought process when it came to considering data and processing states. But the near future is likely to reveal a shocking number of issues related to state machine failures. Possibly coinciding with the uptake of single use microcircuits and the vendor lock-in that goes with that.

Syntactical accuracy & inflexibility - better API security might be enabled by ensuring that a number of parameters that cannot easily be guessed are present in each request.

Layered controls – defence in depth is always a good idea but some of the security standards have not included maturity figures and therefore company are assuming they have all risks adequately covered. When they might have them covered but not adequately. I do not see this position changing. Some companies may decide to take it upon themselves to grow maturity.

Continuous state of security – supply chains in the open market have struggled against a number of factors in the past ten years. If anything, security has declined slightly with the increase of online markets. I am writing this book on a laptop bought from an online market (the biggest one), which I may not have been able to afford if I had bought it elsewhere. But whilst changing out the old SSD drive inside I saw a number of electronic reworks, that got me thinking whether remote control had been added, or whether it was just an electronics fix. Either way, it has not stopped me writing this book. I would have thought by now, that a company would come along and provided a device checking service, for those who want to invest in recycled equipment but are concerned about being spied on. It does not bother us, and we have not been impacted to our knowledge. Is this the reality though?

Immutable infrastructure – some cloud systems are already using immutable builds. That do not allow any interactive human access and are resilient to unauthorised changes by malware. This is likely to continue with the rise in popularity of software pipeline delivery (CI/CD) and Infrastructure as Code (IaC) scripting, like Terraform and Cloudformation. That can enable the creating of new virtual servers and databases in the cloud, without the need to login to the cloud provider's console. The changes are all done using a service account through an API secret key. There are technologies that have been "fire or forget" and we may see more of those appearing, as IoT becomes even more well received. Low-cost items that will work in the way intended, or fail if misused, never to work again. Think about a soda can ring pull, or a firework. It either works or you have to throw it away. Unless you are into blood sports. Any parents will have learnt that lesson.

Controls proportionate to risk – unfortunately, this is less likely to increase in the future. We have seen consumer IoT being used in large organisations, as a replacement for commercial industrial control. Secure IoT device ranges for business use, may start to appear and become more common. As overall, IT transforms through an increase in IoT. But when looking at company IT across the IT industry. It is unlikely at this stage, that control maturity will find its way into security management, at a significant rate. Security controls maturity is generally not marketed as a sales feature. It is considered obscure and something that only very large organisations talk about internally. Suppliers generally do not provide this information. I sadly cannot see this position changing and I cannot see the IoT vendors pushing the agenda.

Data durability & permanence – when working in government, it was tempting whilst all the information was being leaked onto Wikileaks, to have a quick look and see if that piece of information you had requested internally was conveniently online. Of course, I would never do something like that. Going back more than ten years, we did not have the same ubiquity of data that is available now. I can only think that the online availability of your data will become more widely dispersed and more available to you. This is a bit presumptuous. The resurgence of text-based malware in the past couple of years may cause difficulties for some data analytics providers. But this is likely to be in keeping with the expansion of exploits across the industry. Taking offline backups has lost favour with a lot of online service providers recently. If you rely on cloud resilience, there are SLAs and figures to back you up under normal conditions. But if the additional backup copy is administered using the same account, the hackers could delete both online copies of the data. It is an awkward and sometimes difficult practice to get into making offline backups. Some banks have been implementing a wallet system for a number of years, which is bit like a safety deposit box. You drop the wallet through the hole in the wall slot after hours and they make sure it goes in

Conclusions

the safe. Use two banks and USB flash drives, one for the offline backups and one for the password(s). For databases you could try something like:

If you have an unstructured collection of documents in a file share. Search for documents since the last backup. Download them to a staging location.

If you have some data in a database...
"SELECT * from table WHERE record_date > last_backup;"

If you want to get everything, you could use your backup utility, this works even in the cloud with some databases. I have used mysqldump with RDS/MySQL in AWS and this worked well.

You could group the backup files into an archive file using tar and then compress the tar file using gzip, bzip, or xz. After having thought about whether you actually need to back that data up.

On the staging location, using Linux or Windows WSL, something like:
"openssl enc -aes128 -pbkdf2 -in file.txt -out file.aes128"

Enter a complex password that you could generated with:
"openssl rand -hex 32"

To decrypt the file
"openssl enc -aes128 -pbkdf2 -d -in file.aes128 -out file.txt -pass pass:<password>"

Make sure you wipe all the temporary staging documents using
"wipe -qQ1r //tmp//my_folder",
or "dd if=/dev/zero of=/tmp/my_folder"

All of the above commands have been generally correct for over a decade, unless I have made a mistake. Check the online documentation first.

Familiarity – unfortunately, systems are becoming more transitory and vastly more complex. With the increased use of containers and serverless cloud. Serverless compute may run for only a few seconds and then disappear and there may be a whole variety of container applications, scaled to their thousands. Some level of familiarity will always be possible with those who have special attention to detail and a mind that can take it all in. But in general familiarity will be something that we will have to overlay on the IT of the future. "Show me the code" may be replaced with "show me the aggregated machine learning bias graphic".

Observability and transparency of actions – observability has taken a dive in recent years. You would think that with all the movement of IT system to cloud hosting, that comes with log analytics built-in, that it would have increased. Unfortunately, there was a trend in security log management to not prune or discard unnecessary logs and just collect everything. Even though it is actually very simple to search for the top list of events and block them from being stored. Cloud storage costs money. Not a lot. But the cost of storing logs has always been seen as inferior to keeping finance or research data, in terms of the data's value to the organisation. So the choice comes as whether logs should be kept and in a lot of cases, the logging is not switched on, or does not include applications. As I explained in the introduction, log management has been at the heart of cyber operations since the beginning. We may be heading into a future where it is impossible to investigate crimes because there are no audit logs of what happened. The criminal evidence auto-disappears. How convenient for the criminals.

Compensating controls – setting up automated runbooks to augment alerts is already something that is seen with technologies like Security Operations Automation and Response (SOAR) tools. These take events and alerts from a log management system and other security tools and fill in the blanks with contextual information, to do a lot of the basic legwork that a security analyst used to have to do. It is also able to react to alerts and intervene to prevent the escalation of incidents. New products are emerging that are more cloud native, or sympathetic and with the right encouragement could mean that these company products could become more widely used. They may even be acquired and built into the cloud providers platforms. It is more likely that they stay as very expensive marketplace add-ins.

Contain the threat – even modest sized organisations use a vast array of online services, that have a range of different requirements for account management. Trying to contain a threat when all of your eggs are not in one basket is not straightforward. Just this week, there was an incident in the news where the technology provider had been hacked and they had contained the issue and recovered but it turned out that they had not reset the user passwords for a small number of accounts and as a consequence had a follow-up incident where the hackers had monopolised on the foothold that remained. This probably caused more reputation damage than the initial incident, which I was not consciously aware of. Being able to do incident response planning, simulations, or tabletop exercises with dozens of online SaaS provider services is a difficult ask. I think there is room for a standardised protocol (similar to 'Mayday' in aeronautics) to allow a company to immediately contain a threat across a large range of platforms.

System recovery - cloud environments propose a

compelling idea that it is possible to completely rebuild your systems every day from scratch if you want to. I have come across some systems recently that are rebuilt every week. So recovering from a threat, has to do with removing persistent malware. A complete rebuild from clean media should fix that. Of course, this is just from the customer perspective. The cloud providers environment is complex but very well hardening. A clear atrium where any disorder can be immediately remedied. I do not know and there are probably very few people in the world who actually do. The other pervasive aspects of recovery, such as changing account passwords and checking offline backups. There is also still a dependence on admin laptops. So, the threat recovery is not going to greatly improve against a growing threat, unless the client-side attacks are addressed. The admin is now becoming the weakest link.

Soothsaying – putting yourself out there and trying to make a difference can be very dangerous in an industry that is trying to keep shop when so many criminal groups and powerful threat actors are at large. Some names of security researchers, like Aaron Swartz, Dan Kaminsky and Barnaby Jack. Who are sadly no longer with us and died for one reason, or another. Contributed to the history of security and privacy by speaking out about things that they considered to be in the public interest. For some, the need to engage others is a natural progression of something that has been developing for a number of years. For myself, I gave my first talk to a group of fifty salespeople on the subject of IBM SNA (pre-Ethernet) networks in 1993. But it took until 2022 to speak at an international conference. Some might think that is slow progress. Yes, you might be right. Say what you need to say, when you need to say it. But be aware that some opinions are very expensive.

Public communications – this idea is very much tied in

with the current way that we receive information. Over the past ten years, social media has risen and matured. Some areas have even waned. How organisations speak to the public has also become a more mature set of rules, some might even say a science. Getting inside the mind of the recipient, psychologically measuring the sentiment. Ensuring that Search Engine Optimisation (SEO) scores go up, or down. In favour of how you want the message to be received. The IT security industry will need to keep in step with social media, in order to manage security incidents well.

Security training & guidance – training is an area that has changed dramatically over the decades. Once you had to be involved with the security services, military or law enforcement to get any decent security training. That would usually involve classroom training with an instructor. But more recent trends mean that most of the learning comes in snippets of information gathered from social media, security news websites, official notifications for vulnerabilities and such like. The are also lots of free online analysis, courses and YouTube videos. The rise of GenAI will mean that getting an explanation about anything will be as easy as hovering over the question mark on the page and GenAI will fill you in on exactly what you wanted to know.

System documentation – keep documenting everything, it speeds up the support process and it also makes you a better person. There was a spate of network discovery tools that were being marketed before the rise of cloud. I knew a couple of colleagues who engaged their services, one was not satisfied with the outcome if I remember. The other was actually very happy that they did not have to do the hard work of having to check all the facts and put them into a document that could be exported offline. Now with cloud, a lot of those tools are baked in and can make it very easy to map out what you have. Another tool that allows you to model software processes and classes, is Umbrello on Linux. It has been around for a long time, is part of the KDE project which is at the root of everything useful and is excellent at taking an existing codebase and creating a UML model of all the classes and method calls for languages such as C++ and Java. As well as the structure of other web languages.

Testing and vulnerability disclosure - when I was a child, my brother and I used to balance coins on the outside of our elbow and moving the hand palm down swiftly, tried to catch the coins before they hit the floor. We would compete to see how many coins we could catch. But eventually, the coins would become as high as the leaning tower of Pisa and go flying everywhere. Usually without breaking anything important. Manual penetration testing is proving a point, that any given system has some points of weakness, or not. The Whitehat hacker simulates what a criminal, or a spy might do, if they were trying to break in. The simulation is not perfect, the hacker skills may be better, or worse than the threat actors that they are trying to impersonate. The pen testers art is closely aligned with the bug bounty programs and security research. With all this trying to break things, we are finding out how good we are at catching coins but maybe breaking things in the process. It is a neat trick but how many times have I heard that it has gone too far? I have spent a number of years penetration testing and spent several months of my own time in 2023 updating my skills to understand all the latest web penetration testing techniques. There is definitely educational value in practical hacking. But trying to align the availability of security training with those we would like to educate to be hackers, is a complex subject and one that could do with another book being written on the subject. Some nation states have made the subject illegal. The enquiring mind that then gets to work on computer security, immediately has something to teach on the subject. Whether or not, they then go on to use it for the wrong reasons that evening. I could draw a parallel with children born as a result of drunken late-night parties, or during times of war. Hackers, like some midnight children are born of adversity. Their craft does not formalise well, and they do not want to share with the feds. My concern is we may lose all contact with Blackhats. And have no way of modelling the reality of threats to business. Instead, we will just be making it up.

Recent developments in first principles

More recently we have seen a few negative principles emerging that are really anti-patterns to play down previous principles that have become ineffective.

Assume compromise – is a relatively new concept and I think it is really helpful in some cases, but it negates something that we all have to rely on and cannot get away from. Which is the safekeeping principles. These are the solid ground that we have to build on. Assume compromise takes the proposition of "assume safekeeping" and says that we should doubt that in all cases. Assuming some compromise is a more balanced psychological view. Obviously, I am not a psychologist, but I think that assuming total compromise is just going to lead to despair. We should assume that some things are still secure but not be complacent. Which is the aim, I think?

Zero trust – is a concept that I think does not make much sense and could be destructive when you think about it. A bit like a contagious mannerism. Trust is the basis of any civilisation. Having no trust is exactly what we should not want. Even in an anarchic society, there are some forms of trust. But having no trust is analogous of a fearful hellish chaos, where everyone is for themselves, and no-one can do anything productive. I realise that is not what is meant by the phrase. But I have heard many people talking about zero-trust, and they start out by saying. "I think what they mean by zero-trust is…". But why should you need to do that? The name of it should describe what it does. I think we would be best to avoid the phrase altogether. Some technology companies who have invested millions in branding their products as zero-trust. To me, it does not make sense as a security concept. Although, I also think the security implementation would definitely make a measured improvement, when done well.

Potential growth technologies areas
There are a number of new areas of IT growth that are worth mentioning in the context of security. This is the way I see it. Venture capital firms could take a very different view and of course it would be wrong to make false assumptions:

- Artificial intelligence tools and encoding databases
- IoT and blockchain
- Homomorphic Encryption
- Dedicated, application specific field arrays for GenAI

The need for disruptive breakthroughs
Visiting trade conferences over the space of a decade, I got talking to many security technology vendors, about their latest signature-based detection tool. Network IDS, Endpoint Protection software, NG-Firewalls. Same thing, in principle, over and over. Find what bad looks like, model it and try to match it. Each technology type has it strengths and weaknesses. All the salespeople are keen to explain the features, advantages and benefits of investing in their product, instead of the one on the next stall. Companies spend hundreds of thousands a year on software. It's big business and I do not want to dismiss the importance of ensuring that doing the '*right thing*' pays off. Those who invest a lot of time and development dollars in the latest security technologies should be rewarded for sticking with doing the '*right thing*'.

Conclusions

But there is a point where the companies pay money to the technology vendors like it's some sort of superstition tax. Where the tech vendors are stuck in a constant loop around refinements of the same kinds of technologies because they sell. The companies keep paying. Where are the mavericks, the innovators, the ones who will try something completely different because it might actually work, to stop attacks for good. The security vendors want to get ahead of their competition and be effective at security, you see how eager they are to expand into new areas. But new technology is sometimes labelled as a novel obscurity and its value is dismissed. I have seen this a lot over twenty years. But quite a lot of the security technology is to facilitate the responsive strategy of "whack-a-mole" that is based on the "good enough" security approach that favours user experience. Coupled with business expediency of "if it's not broken, don't fix it". But all the time, the attacks are getting worse. The hacker hoards are growing by their tens of thousands.

Ransomware outfits have syndicated and streamlined the whole monetization of criminal enterprise. While companies are still paying billions for firewalls and malware protection software, that do little to stop even one of the attacks that makes the headlines every day. The company on the news that was hacked, it had all the latest security software and firewalls. It had ISO27001 industry certification. The game just got ahead of the industry while we were busy adding new features, to an less than fully effective category of products. The IT security industry is still waiting for a disruptive breakthrough. The greatest breakthroughs, in terms of effective security principles being applied. During the short history of defensive IT security, are probably:

- ☐ Software and hardware logging
- ☐ Passwords
- ☐ Antivirus software
- ☐ Enterprise managed access control

- Network IDS
- Bastions and remote access
- SIEM
- Data loss prevention and classifiers
- Full packet capture analysis
- Network access control
- Memory forensics
- Deception technologies
- ML assistance
- Red/Blue teams
- Cloud compliance monitoring
- Cloud mSOC and response automation
- GenAI features

There are probably many more breakthroughs that some would consider major. When you are working in that sector, it is the only thing you can think of. I apologise if I have missed your area out. The details of the specific features of each of these technologies are the refinements and progressions, that actually make a difference. For instance, Endpoint Protection would be nothing without feature improvements, to combat bypasses and new signatures, to detect all the latest threats. Technologies like SIEM have come a long way since the simple log manager. These improvements to existing technologies, account for most of the progress that has been made in IT security over twenty years. Don't get me wrong. I am on the side of the security vendors. I just want to see us progressing to the next stage where we can say with confidence – all our products are hackproof!

ABOUT THE AUTHOR

The jobs:
1992–1996 Cabletron, sales and junior engineer for network switch manufacturer, now dissolved.

1996–1998 Citicorp, Switzerland, Network Technician for the Northern European team

1998–2001 University of Plymouth, England. Computer systems degree and working part-time as desktop support in the University computer labs.

2003–2006 UK Government, network and security administrator for land registration systems

2006–2013 Capgemini, Security Consultant on the London Metropolitan Police Service account, cyber intrusion and response, other assignments included penetration testing and computer forensics for various customers

2013–2015 Agusta Westland, Security Analyst in weapons manufacturing, defence clearance

2015– IBM Security Division, Security Consultant

2015– NATO, Belgium, cyber defence front-line contractor

2016– UK Government, Cabinet Office, information assurance contractor, Gov.uk

2016–2018 Clarks Shoes, global security architecture

2018–2024 Zurich Insurance, Senior Information Security Consultant, group security assessments

Verticals: government, military & defence, law enforcement, banking & finance, utilities & manufacturing, retail. A total of around twenty to thirty organisations, employers, clients and contract assignments. Some have not been listed, as the assignments were commercial in confidence.